Athens in Decline 404–86 B.C.

Athens in Decline 404–86 B.C.

Claude Mossé
Translated from the French by Jean Stewart

Routledge & Kegan Paul
London and Boston

First published in 1973
by Routledge & Kegan Paul Ltd
Broadway House, 68–74 Carter Lane,
London EC4V 5EL and
9 Park Street, Boston, Mass, 02108, U.S.A.
Printed in Great Britain by
Richard Clay (The Chaucer Press) Ltd
Bungay, Suffolk
© Claude Mossé 1973
This translation © Routledge & Kegan Paul 1973
ISBN 0 7100 7649 5
Library of Congress Catalog Card No 73-81598

Contents

Illustrations

Plates

Maps

Acknowledgments

The author and publishers are grateful to the Loeb Classical Library for permission to reprint passages from Isokrates, *Speeches*, translated by George Norlin and Plutarch, *Lives*, translated by Bernadette Perrin.

Introduction

The history of Athens is a subject of absorbing interest, which has never ceased to arouse impassioned controversy. At different times and from different points of view it has been cited as a model of moderate democracy, of humanism triumphant, or, on the contrary, as an illustration of the disorders due to demagogy or the misdeeds of imperialism. The historian, however, must look beyond appearances in an attempt to understand the exceptional destiny of this Greek city, which for two centuries dominated the Eastern Mediterranean world, which gave birth to a literature of singular richness, which was the home of Aeschylus, Sophocles and Euripides, Aristophanes and Thucydides, Plato and Epicurus, Pheidias and Praxiteles, and which then faded abruptly from the political scene, while Rome set its powerful imprint over the whole Mediterranean.

The origins of Athens were humble. In the Mycenean period the Acropolis was occupied by a 'palace' of modest dimensions. The site continued to exist during the Dark Ages, and the great Dipylon funerary vases bear witness to the existence of a warlike aristocracy ruling over a dependent peasant population. This aristocracy formed the Areopagus, from which were elected the magistrates between whom the former royal power was shared out: the three archons, one of whom still bore the title of *basileus*, the polemarch who presided over affairs of war and the eponymous archon who was responsible for passing judgment.

Towards the end of the seventh century the history of Athens emerges from obscurity. Certain changes, whose nature we cannot clearly discern, resulted in the legislation which we associate with the name of Drakon and the creation of the College of Nomothetes. The attempt of a young aristocrat, Kylon, to assume the tyranny is evidence that Athens was not immune from the broad movement of unrest which at the time disturbed the Aegean world. But it was at the dawn of the sixth century that the crisis broke out which was to decide the future of Athens. Under pressure from the peasant *demos*, the archon Solon took a number of measures intended to put an end to the state of crisis and the threat of revolution it fostered: the suppression of enslavement for debt, and of the dependent state of the peasantry, the codifying and publication of laws, the reform of weights and measures, and the institution of a census aimed at the more equitable distribution of duties, in particular with respect to military burdens and obligations. Contrary to what the Athenians were later to assert, Solon did not create the organs of democracy, but by freeing the peasant from his dependent state he created the social conditions which were to ensure the triumph of democracy. At the time, however, he did not solve the major problem, which was the unequal distribution of the land. The tyrant Peisistratos, however, while satisfying the immediate material demands of the *demos*, completed the work of Solon in the economic sphere by encouraging the development of craftsmanship and mine-working, and by deliberately directing Athenian policy towards the Northern Aegean and towards sources of grain supplies.

But although the path of Athens' future expansion was thus already traced, her social structures remained shackled by ancient bonds of kinship. Kleisthenes was to deal a death-blow to the aristocratic structure of society when he replaced the four Ionian tribes by ten new territorial tribes among which the citizens of Athens were divided, and instituted the *Boule*, the Council whose members, chosen by lot each year in a ratio of fifty for each tribe, constituted a direct expression of the sovereign *demos*.

The lines were now laid down along which the institutions of Athenian democracy were to develop during the fifth century. True, in the first years of that century, the highest posts in the magistracy— the office of archon and, from the Persian wars onwards, of *strategos* —were still held by the representatives of the old aristocratic families. But the *demos* made its weight felt increasingly in assemblies, which now met more frequently and more regularly. The Persian wars, moreover, enabled the urban *demos*, the *thetes* who comprised the crews of warships, to become the decisive factor; and although until about 460 B.C. Athenian policy was still directed by the aristocratic Kimon, who laid the basis of the future Athenian empire, the setbacks which marked the close of his political career allowed Ephialtes to secure the passing of a series of laws which deprived the former aristocratic council of the Areopagus of a large part of its powers, which now devolved upon the Kleisthenian *Boule*. The murder of Ephialtes did not interrupt the evolution thus begun. Perikles, who succeeded him at the head of what may already be described as the democratic party, was to complete the work of Kleisthenes by instituting salaries for public office. At the same time Athens was asserting her hegemony throughout the Aegean, and this enabled the Athenian *demos* to ensure its subsistence by establishing control over the sea routes along which wheat was brought from the Euxine, and to live on the pay ensured by ever-closer surveillance of the allies of Athens. Then a political equilibrium was established which, under the enlightened direction of Perikles, enabled Athenian civilization to blossom. The reconstruction of the sanctuaries destroyed by the Persians on the Acropolis, to which part of the tribute levied from the allies was allocated, brought to Athens the most accomplished craftsmen, the most celebrated artists, and Perikles could justly claim that Athens had become the school of Greece. Such a balance, however, was made possible only by the exercise of increasingly heavy pressure on the allies, and their attempts to evade it were met with harsh repression. Thucydides is justified in recognizing in these excesses of Athenian imperialism the origin of the conflict which was to rend the Greek world for more than a quarter of a century.

In a very short space of time, in fact, the Peloponnesian war was to shatter the balance achieved in the mid-fifth century. The plague, the havoc wrought by Lacedaemonian troops on Athenian territory, the disastrous Sicilian expedition, brought about increased disaffection with the regime. It is thus not surprising that in 411 B.C. the democracy was overthrown by a group of conspirators who had succeeded in creating an atmosphere of fear and insecurity within the city-state. The reaction of the sailors and soldiers of the fleet lying at Samos caused this enterprise to fail: in 410 B.C. democracy was restored and a supreme effort was made to win a decisive victory. Meanwhile, however, Sparta, the principal adversary of Athens, had succeeded, thanks to Persian gold, in creating a powerful navy, and it was at sea that Athens, in 405, suffered the gravest defeat in her history. The starving city, betrayed by those who, led by the Spartan Lysander, were seeking once again to overthrow the democracy, capitulated in September 404 and agreed to hand over her fleet and destroy her walls. Xenophon tells us: 'After this Lysander sailed

3

into Piraeus, the exiles returned, and the people with great enthusiasm began to tear down the walls to the music of flute-girls, thinking that that day was the beginning of freedom for Greece' (*Hellenica*, II, iii, 23).

Yet the history of Athenian democracy does not end there; fortunately for the historian, who would know little or nothing about it if he had to rely only on fifth-century sources, Athenian democracy was to experience another three-quarters of a century of greatness, and to survive, more or less mutilated, under Macedonian domination. It is of the highest interest to the historian to examine the reasons for the final collapse, and to follow the stages of a decline which was not devoid of grandeur. This we shall attempt to do in the following pages.

1 Athens after the end of the Peloponnesian war

Athens emerged from the Peloponnesian war defeated and humiliated. She had lost her foreign possessions, surrendered her fleet, destroyed her Long Walls. She was dependent for her corn supplies on the goodwill of her conqueror, Lysander. It is therefore not surprising that the opponents of democracy, who had been waiting ever since 410 to take their revenge, promptly seized the opportunity offered them.

The political crisis: the oligarchic revolution and the restoration of democracy

The chronology of the events which then took place is not very certain, for our sources sometimes contradict one another. From Xenophon's account it would seem that the establishment of the regime of the Thirty preceded the taking of Samos by Lysander, whereas Lysias in the speech *Against Eratosthenes* seems to suggest that the oligarchs waited to act until the Spartan leader's return.[1] In any case he was present at the Assembly at which the government of the *polis* was handed over to the Thirty. Xenophon merely describes the event as a decision emanating from the people. Lysias, on the contrary, reports strong opposition:

> Theramenes now rose and ordered the city to be put into the hands of thirty individuals, and the constitution in preparation by Drakontides to be adopted. Even as things were, there was a violent outburst in refusal. It was realised that the issue of the meeting was slavery or freedom. Theramenes, as members of the jury can themselves testify, declared that he cared nothing for this outburst, as he knew that a large number of Athenians were in favour of the same

5

measures as himself, and he was voicing the decisions approved by Sparta and Lysander. After him Lysander spoke, and among other statements pronounced that he held Athens under penalty for failing to carry out the terms of the truce, and that the question would not be one of her constitution, but of her continued existence. True and loyal members of the Assembly realised the degree to which the position had been prepared and compulsion laid upon them, and either stood still in silence or left, with their conscience clear at any rate of having voted the ruin of Athens (*Against Eratosthenes*, 73–5).

This implies that a small minority of those present had been solely responsible for deciding the city's fate. We may, of course, wonder whether Lysias, prosecuting one of the Thirty some years after the event, did not find it advantageous to flatter the judges by absolving them of responsibility and praising their resistance, however passive. In point of fact, if we are to believe another of Lysias' speeches, *Against Agoratos*, the leading democrats had already been arrested or had gone into exile on the conclusion of the peace treaty. However that may be, thirty citizens were thus appointed whose mission was to draw up a new constitution, or rather a constitution conforming to the *patrios politeia*, the ancestral constitution.[2] The only information we possess on the manner in which the Thirty were appointed is provided by Lysias, in the same speech *Against Eratosthenes* (76): ten of them were appointed by Theramenes, who does indeed seem, in collusion with Lysander, to have instigated the whole affair; ten more by the ephors, and the last ten elected by what remained of the Assembly. These thirty evidently included Theramenes, Kritias, Plato's cousin, who had had a stormy political career during the closing years of the Peloponnesian war, Drakontides, Peison and other less-known figures, among them Lysias' future adversary, Eratosthenes. Their first concern was to appoint a Council composed of their supporters and to make sure of controlling the principal magistrates' colleges. Next they brought to trial before the Council a certain number of citizens who had previously been arrested on a charge of plotting against the safety of the state, but in actual fact, if we are to believe the author of the speech *Against Agoratos* (15 ff.), for having tried to oppose the peace treaty which reduced Athens to unconditional surrender. We may assume that these summary sentences, imposed under illegal conditions, aroused some dissatisfaction, and that in order to have their hands free the

Thirty then asked Sparta to send a Lacedaemonian garrison. Xenophon tells us:

> Once they had got the garrison, they paid court to Callibios in every way, in order that he might approve of everything they did, and as he detailed guardsmen to go with them, they arrested the people whom they wished to reach—not now the 'scoundrels' and persons of little account, but from this time forth the men who, they thought, were least likely to submit to being ignored, and who, if they undertook to offer any opposition, would obtain supporters in the greatest numbers (*Hellenica*, XI, iii, 14).

In the speech *Against Eratosthenes* Lysias gives us an example of this kind of summary arrest:

> At a meeting of the Thirty, Theognis and Peison made a statement that some of the metics were disaffected, and they saw this as an excellent pretext for action which would be punitive in appearance, but lucrative in reality. They had no difficulty in persuading their fellows, to whom killing was nothing, while money was of great importance. They therefore decided to arrest ten people, including two of the poorer class, to enable them to claim that their object was not money, but the good of others, as in any other respectable enterprise (*Against Eratosthenes*, 6–7).

The Thirty therefore shared out the task among themselves, and it was Peison and Theognis who entered the house where Lysias was dwelling. While Theognis went into the factory which Lysias had inherited from his father, Kephalos, to make an inventory of the slaves and of the objects there, Lysias succeeded in 'buying off' Peison, who took him to the house of a mutual friend, whence Lysias was able to escape through an unguarded door and reach the port, where he succeeded in embarking for Megara. Meanwhile another of the Thirty, Eratosthenes, had seized Polemarchos, brother of Lysias, and taken him to prison, where he was made to drink hemlock. The Thirty were now free to seize the fortune of the two brothers, their furniture and jewels and clothes and the hundred and twenty slaves who were working in the factory.

There can be no doubt that such scenes took place repeatedly, spreading terror in the city among all those whose wealth or whose opinions made them suspect to the masters of the hour. According to Xenophon and Aristotle,[3] it was these arbitrary measures which brought about the rupture between Theramenes, who had hitherto been seen as the leader of the Thirty, and Kritias. This tradition, favourable to Theramenes, which we find expressed by Xenophon and by Aristotle in particular, must have arisen immediately after the restoration of the democracy, and it is interesting to note that Lysias, in the speech *Against Eratosthenes*, attacks those who tried to make Theramenes out as a victim:

> If the friends of Theramenes had perished with him, unless they had adopted the opposite course to his, it would have been no more than they deserved. Instead of this we find a defence made of him, and attempts by his associates to take credit as the authors of numerous benefits instead of untold detriment (64).

And Lysias reminds his hearers that Theramenes had been one of the Four Hundred, and that after Aigospotamoi it was he who, by dragging out negotiations, had helped to deliver Athens into the hands of Lysander. In the eyes of the democrats, Theramenes was the accomplice of the oligarchs. For a whole section of Athenian opinion, however, he represented a moderate trend, as foreign to the demagogy of the last years of the war as to the extreme oligarchy of which Kritias was the representative. And the profession of faith attributed to him by Xenophon in the *Hellenica*, during his famous debate with Kritias, is a fair summary of the 'programme' of these moderates:

> But I, Kritias, am forever at war with the men who do not think there could be a good democracy until the slaves and those who would sell the state for lack of a shilling should share in the government, and on the other hand I am forever an enemy to those who do not think that a good oligarchy could be established until they should bring the state to the point of being ruled absolutely by a few. But to direct the government in company with those who have the means to be of service, whether with horses or with shields,—this plan I regarded as best in former days and I do not change my opinion now (*Hellenica*, II, iii, 48).

In point of fact, even if we are to accept as authentic the opposition between the extremist and the moderate trends of the oligarchic 'party', it was clearly in the interest of Theramenes' friends, so soon after the restoration of the democracy, to stress that opposition, distinguishing themselves from Kritias and his accomplices. None the less the rupture between Kritias and Theramenes, and the death sentence passed on the latter, under illegal conditions, reflected divergences within the oligarchic class, divergences which were to contribute to the weakening of the regime of the Thirty.

For while the city endured a reign of terror which entailed many arrests, banishments and confiscations of goods, resistance was beginning to be organized. It was probably soon after the arrest and execution of Theramenes that Thrasyboulos, who had taken refuge in Thebes, succeeded with a small band of supporters in seizing the citadel of Phyle. This first success was to have important consequences. Supporters poured in from all parts of Attica, and soon Thrasyboulos was strong enough to launch an attack on the horsemen who had been sent by Kritias into the frontier region between Boiotia and Attica. The result of this military success was not only to strengthen the position of the democrats but, furthermore, to alarm the Thirty, who left Athens and took refuge at Eleusis, having first put to death all those whom they considered suspect, both at Eleusis and at Salamis.

The gulf grew even wider between the oligarchic extremists and the townspeople, most of whom were inscribed on the list of the Three Thousand, and who had begun to envisage a *rapprochement* with the people of Phyle. Soon afterwards, Thrasyboulos, the number of whose supporters had constantly increased, took possession of the Piraeus. The Thirty made a last effort to recapture the port, but they were defeated at Munychia in a battle in which Kritias lost his life. Confusion reigned among the oligarchs. They were divided as to the course to be followed. Some, more clear-sighted, realizing that it would not be easy to recapture the port, were in favour of reconciliation with Thrasyboulos; others 'urged strenuously that they ought not to yield to the men of the Piraeus' (*Hellenica*, II, iv, 23). Finally the people of the city, dismissing the Thirty to Eleusis for good, appointed ten magistrates, among whom were some men who might be expected to work for reconciliation with the democrats. At all events, this is what Lysias implies in the speech *Against Eratosthenes*. But, the orator adds, 'as soon as they assumed power themselves they gave rise to still more violent dissension in Athens, against the Piraeus. . . . On assuming control of the government and the city, they made common cause against the Thirty who had been the cause, and the people's party who had been the victims, of all the trouble' (57).

In fact, the war began again more fiercely than ever between the two sides. On the Piraeus, Thrasyboulos mobilized forces of every sort. It is interesting to note that, in view of the political character of the struggle, he did not merely recruit men of every social condition

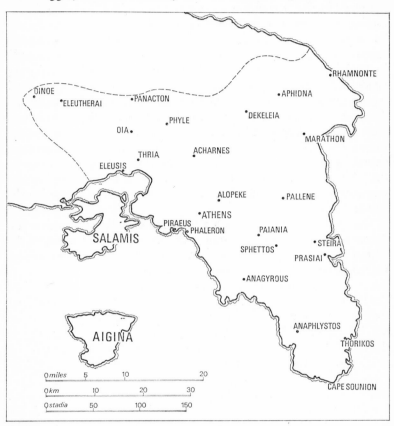

Attica

to fight side by side, he even appealed to foreigners, promising them *isoteleia* if they would engage in battle by the citizens' side. We have here an even clearer indication than in 411 B.C. that political oppositions did in fact conceal social antagonisms, and that the presence of rich men in Thrasyboulos' party did not invalidate the popular character of his army, in which light infantry, armed with hastily improvised bucklers, replaced the heavy infantry of the hoplites, and which included few horsemen. The townspeople took fright on see-ing these developments, and appealed to Lysander to intervene without delay. He therefore prepared to concentrate his forces at Eleusis and to block the port so as to prevent supplies from reach-ing the Piraeus. Xenophon's account gives one the impression that without the intervention of the Spartan king, Pausanias, who, jealous of Lysander, decided to take him by surprise and to negotiate peace between the two parties, the men of Piraeus would have been doomed to defeat. Xenophon himself admits, however, that Thrasyboulos succeeded in repulsing the assault made jointly by Pausanias' army and Lysander's mercenaries against the Piraeus, and that this victory precipitated negotiations. And it was indeed as victors that the men of Piraeus returned to Athens and climbed the Acropolis 'in arms' to sacrifice to the goddess. The only result of Pausanias' good offices was the undertaking made by the democrats not to seek vengeance on their adversaries except in the case of those who had compromised themselves with the oligarchy. The speech ascribed by Xenophon to Thrasyboulos at the end of Book III of the *Hellenica* is clear evidence of the political character of the victory won by the democrats. The victor's words are first addressed to the townspeople, challenging the superiority on which they prided themselves in order to claim an exclusive right to political power:

Are you more just? But the commons, though poorer than you, never did you any wrong for the sake of money; while you, though richer than any of them, have done many disgraceful things for the sake of gain. But since you can lay no claim to justice, consider then whether it is courage that you have a right to pride yourselves upon. And what better test could there be of this than the way we made war upon one another? Well then, would you say that you are superior in intelligence, you who, having a wall, arms, money, and the Peloponnesians as allies, have been worsted by men who had none of these? (II, iv, 40-1).

Then Thrasyboulos, addressing his comrades-in-arms, urged them to respect their vows and indulge in no revolutionary agitation, but on the contrary to return to the ancient laws of the *polis*. Are we to suppose that, under cover of the conflict, certain men were aiming at something more than the mere restoration of democracy? It is almost impossible to answer this question, since no other source refers to any sort of disturbance. May we assume that certain exiles, on their return to Athens, wished to dispossess their adversaries of the goods these had acquired more or less justly, and to proceed to large-scale confiscations, even to a redistribution of the land, as was being done and would continue to be done elsewhere? The only 'illegal' measures seem to have been those proposed by Thrasyboulos in favour of the foreigners and slaves who had fought by his side, on whom he wanted to confer the right of citizenship. A *graphe paranomon* was brought against him by Archinos, and the proposal was dropped.[4]

We may wonder why the Athenian *demos* consented so readily to be cheated of the material advantages of victory, and why, during the years that followed, the city-state was in fact ruled by the most moderate members of the Piraeus party, such as Archinos and Anytos, in conjunction with the townspeople. Several answers are possible. Some may argue from the prudence and moderation characteristic of the Athenian people; others will stress the social power of the rich, who, though politically divided, were united in defence of order. It is possible, however, that an analysis of the material situation of Athens immediately after the war will provide the data for a more satisfactory explanation.

The economic crisis: the destitution of the peasantry,
the new rich, and the urban *demos*

The Peloponnesian war had been a particularly harsh ordeal for Athens. The epidemic of plague at the beginning of the war had drastically reduced her population. The Sicilian disaster had also dealt the Athenians a severe blow. We know how hard it is to make a precise estimate of the population of Attica, for figures are scarce and fragmentary. But those cited by Thucydides concerning the military forces of Athens at the beginning of the war have enabled certain modern historians to reckon the number of citizens of Attica, towards 431 B.C., at about 40,000.[5] Now two indications at the beginning of the fourth century suggest that there had been a noticeable drop in this civic population: Plato in the *Symposium* (175e) and Aristophanes in the *Ekklesiazusae* (*Women in the Assembly*) (l. 1132) give the same figure of 30,000 Athenians. This implies that the war had deprived Athens of about a quarter of her citizens.

These very considerable losses in human lives were due to various factors: the plague, as we have seen, but also military operations, defeat in Sicily, and the political troubles of the end of the fifth century. It is also possible that the loss of certain cleruchies had entailed a decrease in the civic body: many cleruchs must have chosen to renounce their status as Athenians rather than the land which provided their living.

In addition to these human casualties, the country suffered severe devastation. Attica had been invaded several times during the first part of the war, usually known as the war of Archidamos. But the harshest blows were inflicted after 412 B.C., when a Spartan garrison had been permanently established at Dekeleia. From this base the Lacedaemonians could sally forth on continual raids, destroying harvests and pillaging. The country districts were of course the worst affected by these operations. All contemporary texts refer to the distress of Athens in the immediate post-war period. Perhaps the most striking of these are Aristophanes' two last comedies, the *Ekklesiazusae* and the *Ploutos*. The *Ekklesiazusae*, performed in 392 B.C., that is to say some ten years after the end of the war, is a farcical comedy in which Aristophanes imagines the women of Athens, weary of the men's bad government, seizing power by craft. The interesting thing about the play is that, having taken control of the state, the women proclaim that henceforward all possessions are to be held in common. This total communism is intended to bring to an end the shameful inequality of fortunes and the destitution of the majority. The same problem of the inequality of fortunes and the poverty of the people is referred to again in Aristophanes' last play, the *Ploutos*, performed four years after the *Ekklesiazusae*, in 388 B.C. When Chremylos, the hero of the play, who has restored his sight to Ploutos, god of Wealth, addresses Poverty, he describes the ills which she has inflicted on men:

What good can you bring except for burns endured at the baths, starving children and a whole swarm of old women? As for the number of fleas, lice and gnats, they are too many to mention, buzzing round our heads, teasing us, waking us up and telling us: 'You're hungry, come on, get up.' Yes, and besides all that, to have a rag for a cloak, a litter of rushes for a bed, full of bugs that keep one from sleeping, with a rotten straw mat for a carpet, and a big stone under one's head for a pillow; to eat mallow stalks instead of bread, and dry radish-leaves instead of cake; with the top of a broken pot to sit

13

on, and the side of a smashed-in cask to serve as kneading-trough; yes, haven't I shown you that these are the blessings you bring to mankind? (l. 540 ff.).

Athenian writers at the beginning of the century echo the words of Aristophanes and, like him, stress the damage wrought by war and the increasing sufferings of the majority of the people. The speeches of Lysias, composed during the years that followed the restoration of democracy, are eloquent in this respect. The orator contrasts the rapid enrichment of the few with the poverty and misery of the many. In the oration *On the Sacred Olive Tree* (33) he dwells particularly on the distress of the countryside during the war: ravaged fields, uprooted trees, confiscated lands that lie fallow for years for lack of a purchaser, or in a short space of time are handed on from one farmer to another . . . Now in this particular case, the plaintiff was a rich man who owned several properties in the Paedeion. He had none the less suffered severely through the war, since part of his olive groves had been burnt down.

The distress of the countryside, indeed, did not affect the poor peasants alone. Well-off landowners, too, had to face increased difficulties. Certain dialogues in Xenophon's *Memorabilia* refer to these hardships, which obliged respectable Athenians to resort to all sorts of expedients in order to live. One man might be forced to set the women of his family to work, since he could not feed useless mouths; another might take a post as steward to a more fortunate neighbour.[6] There were undoubtedly some cases of neglected lands, of which certain speculators took advantage: the operations indulged in by the father of Ischomachos, the wealthy landowner of Xenophon's *Oeconomicus*,[7] are assuredly an example of this sort of speculation, which must have gone on during the post-war years. Does this, however, imply the beginning of peasant indebtedness and the concentration of estates, as has sometimes been said? An analysis of fourth-century hypothecation boundary marks has shown that these were seldom connected with small properties.[8] The systematic study of texts has made it possible to prove that at least during the first half of the fourth century landed property in Attica was parcelled out to a considerable extent. Poverty in the countryside was none the less a real fact, at least during the first decades of the century, when a state of war was practically endemic and the threat of foreign invasion still hung over Attica.

But war did not affect Athenian agriculture alone. Mining, one of Athens' most important activities, on which her prosperity in part depended, was equally hard hit.

The Laurion mines, indeed, provided the Athenian state with the silver used in the manufacture of the precious 'owls' which were much sought after throughout the Aegean world and beyond, in the West and in the barbarian East. Practically nothing is known of the laws controlling mining in the fifth century, since most of our epigraphical documentation dates from the second half of the fourth century. And Aristotle's analysis in the *Constitution of Athens* refers solely to the reorganization generally attributed to Kallistratos (cf. below, page 43). We only know that a large number of slaves belonging to private individuals were employed there to extract the ore. Thus Nikias, the famous and unfortunate *strategos* of the Sicilian expedition, had a thousand slaves employed in the mines, each of whom earned for him one obol a day. The occupation of Dekeleia by the Spartans had disastrous consequences for the mining industry. Thucydides refers to the flight of 20,000 artisan slaves, and it is generally believed that most of these were miners. Xenophon in *Ways and Means*, written about 356, insists strongly on the disastrous consequences which the war had had on the mining industry. Many galleries had been abandoned, and the authorities were reluctant to reopen them or to start working new ones. We know too little, unfortunately, about the laws of the Athenian economy and the part played in it by money to assess the precise effects on that economy of this slowing-down of the mining industry. In any case, the commercial difficulties of Athens must have increased markedly, particularly with regard to supplies. Of course, here again, we have to argue from a few fragmentary indications. It appears undeniable, however, that in the years following the restoration of the democracy Athens had great difficulty in ensuring her corn supplies, and ran short of wheat. Speaking of the Spartan peace proposals of 392, through which Sparta recognized the right of Athens to rebuild her walls, a democratic orator declared: 'Walls will not give us food.'⁹

The lawsuit brought by one of Lysias' clients against corn merchants provides further evidence of these difficulties, and also of the speculation to which they gave rise. It is quite clear that they were connected with the obstacles that confronted the Athenians in their attempts to regain a footing in the north of the Aegean, owing to the continued alliance between Sparta and the Great King and his satraps, particularly Tissaphernes. To escape from this dilemma Athens obviously needed a fleet, and to equip this fleet she needed money; but her financial resources were almost non-existent, since the mines were no longer being worked and since, furthermore, the general state of insecurity was keeping traders away from the Piraeus. We can thus understand how the only solution, in many people's eyes, was military revenge, a return to imperialism, war which might bring riches and, at the same time, ensure a regular wage for the *demos*.

It thus becomes easier to understand the twofold antagonism within the city-state: on the one hand between rich and poor, the former seeking to be released from trierarchies and property-taxes, the latter ready to vote in favour of any expedition which might provide them with booty; and on the other hand between country folk disturbed at the prospect of a new war which would be at their expense, and townsfolk anxious to ensure their daily bread and, to that end, hoping to see Athens resume her place in the Straits and in the Northern Aegean. This twofold antagonism is stressed by all contemporary writers of the first years of the fourth century, by Aristophanes as well as by the anonymous historian of the *Hellenica Oxyrhynchia* from Oxyrhynchos, and in the speeches of Andokides and those of Lysias. And it forms a background to the theoretical writings of Plato, particularly the *Republic*, that study of a just *polis*, a model construction free from the antagonisms which, everywhere else, divided cities into two hostile states, that of the rich and that of the poor.[10]

It is noteworthy, however, that although these antagonisms were asserted in assemblies and lawcourts, they did not lead to any real confrontation. Neither on the political nor on the social plane do we witness a crisis comparable with those that Athens had experienced at other times. It is difficult to explain the stability of Athens during the first years of the fourth century, which forms so remarkable a contrast with the disturbed state of other parts of the Greek world. We can discern a number of explanatory factors: the persistence of land-ownership among the small and middle peasantry—at the beginning of the fourth century, only 5,000 Athenians out of a total of 30,000 owned no land[11]—which enabled Athens to avoid the agrarian crisis which was experienced elsewhere; the equipment of the Piraeus, which encouraged traders, in spite of obstacles, to unload their goods there; the attachment of the mass of the *demos* to the regime, and simultaneously a growing indifference towards political affairs, to which the institution of the *misthos ekklesiastikos* by Agyrrhios bears witness; and perhaps, finally, a general weariness which allowed certain clever politicians to manoeuvre and certain clever *strategoi* to act simultaneously on their own behalf and on that of the state. This problem, to which we shall return, shows that the war had left grave after-effects which were not confined to material losses but implied a profound transformation of men's minds.

The moral and religious crisis

Unquestionably, the Peloponnesian war gave rise to a grave moral and religious crisis in Athens which was in no small degree responsible for altering the ethical code of the city-state and which explains certain aspects of Athenian life in the fourth century. It is of course not very easy to assess the importance of that crisis, nor to describe its various features. Thucydides, in his account of the Peloponnesian war, attributed to the plague the origins of the serious moral crisis which affected Athens.

> In other respects also Athens owed to the plague the beginnings of a state of unprecedented lawlessness. Seeing how quick and abrupt were the changes of fortune which came to the rich who suddenly died and to those who had previously been penniless but now inherited their wealth, people now began openly to venture on acts of self-indulgence which before then they used to keep dark. Thus they resolved to spend their money quickly and to spend it on pleasure, since money and life alike seemed equally ephemeral. As for what is called honour, no one showed himself willing to abide by its laws, so doubtful was it whether one would survive to enjoy the name for it. It was generally agreed that what was both honourable and valuable was the pleasure of the moment and everything that might conceivably contribute to that pleasure. No fear of god or law of man had a restraining influence. As for the gods, it seemed to be the same thing whether one worshipped them or not, when one saw the good and the bad dying indiscriminately. As for offences against human law, no one expected to live long enough to be brought to trial and punished: instead everyone felt that already a far heavier sentence had been passed on him and was hanging over him, and that before

the time for its execution arrived it was only natural to get some pleasure out of life (II, 53).

This code of self-indulgence and pleasure at any price was to outlast the epidemic of pestilence. We find it defended, at the beginning of the fourth century, by Kallikles in Plato's *Gorgias*:

Natural fairness and justice, I tell you now quite frankly, is this—that he who would live rightly should let his desires be as strong as possible and not chasten them, and should be able to minister to them when they are at their height by reason of his manliness and intelligence, and satisfy each appetite in turn with what it desires (491e).

And we meet it again in the words of Thrasymachos in the *Republic*. The strong man, the man who is and who feels himself superior to the crowd, is entitled to despise the laws and to follow his passions, since the laws are merely for the protection of the weak. This moral code, which was inherited from one stream of Sophistic teaching, was obviously at variance with the collective ethic presupposed by the city-state's ideal. With its emphasis on the individual, the superior being, it was the very negation of democratic equality. It is not surprising that Kritias supported it. That same Kritias was also the author of a satyr-play, *Sisyphus*, of which only one extract has come down to us, which constitutes a violent criticism of traditional religion: [12]

There was a time when the life of man was disordered and like that of wild beasts controlled by brute strength. There was then no reward for the good nor any punishment for the bad. Next, men conceive the idea of imposing laws as instruments of punishment, so that justice may be sole ruler and hold violence in check. If any erred, he was punished. Then, since the laws only prevented the commission of deeds of *open* violence, men continued to commit secret crimes. At this point it is my belief that some far-seeing and resolute man saw the need for a deterrent which would have effect even when *secret* deeds were done or contemplated. So he introduced the idea of divinity, of a god always active and vigorous, hearing and seeing with his mind . . . all that men say or do. . . . This then was the origin of belief in the gods as well as of obedience to the laws.

Such a conception of the origins of the gods was not widespread. Atheism was an awkward position to hold in Athens, as some men, such as Anaxagoras, had learned by bitter experience. But although religious conformism was an integral part of the democratic ethic, the crisis which the city's religious life was going through was none the less real. It was reflected in particular by an increasing interest in foreign creeds or in certain forms of the worship of the deities traditionally admitted into the Greek pantheon. The introduction into Athens of the cult of the Thracian goddess, Bendis, is one example of these new features of religious life, while the *Bacchae* of Euripides also gives evidence of an unfamiliar type of religious feeling. Faced with the distresses of their time, Athenians sought refuge in mystical cults which offered the promise of a life beyond, and the comfort of communion with the deity. Others tried to find in traditional religion the foundation for an individual morality which was only very loosely connected with the religious practices of the *polis*. Socrates was one of these; turning to account the Delphic maxim, he questioned himself and questioned his disciples in order to bring them to work out an ethical code based on the knowledge of justice. Although he professed to despise the teachers of eloquence who sold their learning, Socrates 'the Sophist' was after all not far removed from those men who in their speeches called in question traditional customs and morality. And this no doubt explains the indictment brought against him by the victorious democrats. In fact, despite the obscurity surrounding the figure of Socrates, whom we know solely through the words of his disciples, we may safely consider that his trial in 399 was not a political one. Socrates had not been involved with the oligarchy. He had even refused to connive at the arrest of the rich man Leon of Salamis, and if he had repeatedly shown that he did not intend to bow to unjust decisions even when they emanated from the sovereign assembly, he had never sought to oppose existing laws. The sayings attributed to him by both Plato and Xenophon are unambiguous on this point.

In other respects, moreover, those who instituted the trial which was to end in his condemnation to death were not democrats eager for vengeance. The chief accuser, the tanner Anytos, was one of Theramenes' friends, and though he eventually sided with Thrasyboulos he none the less represented the moderate, conformist trend. It was, moreover, in the name of that conformism that he accused Socrates of perverting the young and of failing to respect the gods of the *polis*.[13] The trial of Socrates has thus nothing in common with those other trials which, in the years following the restoration of democracy, appear, notwithstanding the law of amnesty, to represent a settling of accounts between 'townspeople' and 'men of the Piraeus', and of which the speeches of Lysias provide evidence. But the severity of his sentence shows how deeply conscious the democratic leaders were of the gravity of the moral and religious crisis, and how determined to check it by a repressive policy. In fact such a policy proved ineffective because it was directed against superficial phenomena without examining their deep-seated causes. And the moral confusion, the disloyalty towards the gods of the *polis* was to increase during the fourth century, in association with that decline of the civic consciousness which reveals the slow break-up of the civic community and heralds the end of the city-state.

2 The rebirth of imperialist democracy (404–359 B.C.)

The situation of Athens immediately after the end of the Peloponnesian war was indeed dramatic, but not so much so as to prevent a retrieval of her fortunes. And this took place in a spectacular fashion during the ensuing years. In a few decades, indeed, Athens, once defeated and humiliated, was to recover her empire in the Aegean, to reconstitute her economic power and, while all her rivals declined, to represent the sole military force capable of offering resistance to Philip of Macedon.

To understand the reasons for this rebirth it is important to consider all its aspects; and primarily to examine the political conditions that prevailed during the upsurge of Athenian imperialism.

New features of political life

In 403 B.C. democracy had been restored; but this did not mean a straightforward return to an earlier system. Aristotle speaks of an eleventh reform (*metabole*) of the Athenian constitution,[1] and this seems to be more than a merely formal expression. A profound revision of the laws took place then. Andokides, in his speech *On the Mysteries*, relates the circumstances which accompanied this revision:

> When . . . you returned from the Piraeus, you were in a position to impose penalties, but you decided to let bygones be bygones, and preferred the preservation of Athens to private revenges, resolving to wipe the slate clean all round. On this decision you elected a board of twenty to administer the city till legislation could be passed. Meanwhile the code of Solon and the enactments of Draco were to hold. But after drawing lots for a Council and electing a

legislative committee you found that a good many of Solon's and Draco's enactments left a number of citizens liable to penalties for former activities. At an assembly on the point, you passed a measure to make an examination of all the laws and inscribe in the Stoa such as were approved (I, 81–2).

Actually a commission of nomothetes had already been set up, in 409 B.C., to undertake a revision of the laws.[2] Its work, however, had been interrupted by the oligarchic revolution. In 403 a decree written by one Tisamenos, who seems to have been one of those clerks who prepared the work of the nomothetes, was adopted by the Assembly; it declared that the revision of the laws would be resumed. This entailed examining the bulk of Solon's legislation and the earlier Drakonian laws and adapting these to the new situation and the altered realities. The work seems to have taken a long time, since in 399 we find a client of Lysias accusing one of the clerks responsible for transcribing the laws of failing to complete, after four years, a task which should have been finished in a few months.[3] It is clear, however, that this revision of the laws entailed no profound alteration of the actual constitution. The *ekklesia* was still the sovereign body and its meetings were held four times in each prytany on the Pnyx. The new feature was the institution of the *misthos ekklesiastikos* by Agyrrhios.[4] This was obviously aimed at combating the absenteeism which was characteristic of the restored democracy, and the rapidity with which it was raised to three obols shows that this was its object. Aristotle, in the *Constitution of Athens*, after going through the eleven reforms of the *politeia*, concludes:

> Eleventh was the constitution established after the return from Phyle and from Piraeus, from which date the constitution has continued down to its present form, constantly taking on additions to the power of the multitude. For the people has made itself master of everything, and administers everything by decrees and by jury-courts in which the people is the ruling power, for even the cases tried by the Council have come to the people. And they seem to act rightly in doing this, for a few are more easily corrupted by gain and by influence than the many (41, 2).

That the omnipotence of the Assembly was a reality is asserted by all contemporary sources, and even more than in the preceding century the art of public speaking became the condition of any political career. Must one, however, follow Aristotle completely when he stresses the Council's loss of power? True, there may have been a certain lingering mistrust of the Council, which had twice been the passive instrument of oligarchic revolution; and it is not impossible that control of certain affairs may have been withdrawn from it. But on the whole it seems still to have played an essential political role in the fourth century. It was responsible for preparing the Assembly's debates, it subjected magistrates, whether elected or drawn by lot, to the *dokimasia* when they assumed office and examined their accounts when they retired. It was from the Council that those specialized commissions were drawn which supervised the sale of confiscated property, the adjudication of mining concessions and the building of ships. The Council received foreign ambassadors and concluded peace treaties. More than ever, and even though its judiciary powers had been curtailed in favour of the courts derived from the Heliaia, it constituted the permanent supreme body of the state.

The fact remains that the courts of the Heliaia tended to assume ever-increasing importance, and the growing number of lawsuits is a characteristic feature of the fourth century which has provided us with an incomparable collection of documents: Athens in the fourth century had become the 'Lawyers' Republic'. This increase in lawsuits, moreover, was not merely a chance occurrence; it reflects both the new conditions of political life and the new economic realities.

Political life in the fourth century, at any rate during the first half of that century, displays a somewhat disconcerting character. One is suddenly aware that the great ideological debates of the late fifth century had been abandoned. True, in the years that followed the restoration of the democracy, the old resentments were not allayed, and the speeches of Lysias show that 'townspeople' and 'men of the Piraeus' continued to mistrust one another despite repeated references to the famous amnesty; but there does not seem to have been any oligarchic 'party' in Athens, nor any sort of threat to the regime. The men who, in 403, dominated the political scene, men such as Archinos or Anytos, were moderates, opposed to any extreme but firmly attached to the restored democracy, and the final attempt made to salvage something from the 'oligarchic' programme, the decree proposed by one Phormisios aimed at limiting the exercise of political rights to owners of landed property, was rejected.[5]

And yet the fifty years that followed the restoration of the democracy were marked by an increase in the number of political trials, aimed essentially at the *strategoi* but incidentally (or by reaction) affecting most prominent political men. Faced with this profusion of political trials, the historian is obviously tempted to enquire into their origin, the forces confronting one another and the real significance of the phenomenon. Were there mutually hostile parties, and were these trials their means of combat? We must pause to consider the various answers that have been given to these questions.

Ancient authors, particularly the political writers of the fourth century, distinguished two antagonistic groups within the *polis*: the poor and the rich, whom they identified in somewhat summary fashion with democrats and oligarchs. Broadly speaking, there is some reality behind this definition. But in Athens, during the first decades of the fourth century, while there were unquestionably rich and poor whose interests sometimes diverged, there were no longer, as we have already pointed out, any self-styled oligarchs. It may therefore be asked how political antagonisms expressed themselves.

The simplest interpretation seems to be based on the attitude of political men towards Sparta and Thebes; in the first decades of the fourth century there appear to have been a 'Spartiate' and a 'Theban' party in Athens. The former comprised those men who, particularly after 386, realized that the struggle for hegemony was futile, that it was no longer possible to return to the practices of the previous century and that the immediate task was to maintain the position of Athens in the Aegean, indispensable in order to ensure her supplies of corn, but on the mainland to accept shared influence with Sparta. It was not a case of unconditional 'lakonophilia' as in the preceding century (and in any case fourth-century Sparta was only a pale shadow of Lykourgos' city) but rather of a pragmatic attitude to things. In opposition to this 'Spartiate' party was a 'Theban' party, led by the men who in 404 had taken refuge in Thebes and who banked on the growing antagonism between Sparta and Thebes to ensure the rebirth of Athenian imperialism. After 379 the democratic revolution in Thebes was to offer this party the hope of revenge and of a final crushing of the hereditary enemy, Sparta. Kallistratos is seen as the representative of one of these two main trends and Aristophon of the other.

This interpretation of the political antagonisms in Athens during the first half of the fourth century is open to a number of objections.

Plate 1 Statue of girl 'Bear' from the temple of Artemis, fourth century B.C.

Plate 2 Relief from basis showing Pyrrhic dancers from the Acropolis Museum, fourth century B.C.

For it must be admitted that there is no clear evidence of devotion to Sparta by one group or to Thebes by another. Some modern historians are therefore inclined to replace this over-simplified explanation by an alternative analysis of the political situation in Athens: the professionalization of political life on the one hand, the abdication of the *demos* on the other.

The increasingly professional character of political life reflects the growth of what may be called the apparatus of state. The Greek *polis* was originally a human community: there was no Athenian state, there were only Athenians. The *polis* retained this character until the end of the Classical epoch, as we see from the headings of treaties, the system of liturgies and the various systems of benefaction. As society became more diversified, however, as the juridical apparatus grew more complicated and economic realities more involved, the need was felt for more specialized skills and for a greater permanency of functions.

True, the 'magistrates', in spite of the salaries they now drew, were not yet 'civil servants', but some of them were tending in that direction. This specialization of functions is obviously in contradiction with the essential spirit of the *polis*, in which every citizen must be able in his turn to govern and to obey, but it was becoming increasingly the rule. Let us consider merely two essential problems which Athens had to face at the beginning of the fourth century: the military problem and the financial problem. War was part of a citizen's normal activities. At any moment he might be called upon to defend his land, and the military organization followed the political organization closely. The *strategos* elected by the *demos* was responsible to the *demos* for his actions, and he could summon an assembly of soldiers in the middle of a campaign. Thucydides cites many examples of such meetings, particularly when the army was at some distance from the city.[6]

Such political practices were not confined to Athens, and it is interesting to find them existing even in such a heterogeneous army as that of the Ten Thousand. At the same time, precisely because that army was composed of mercenaries, it gave rise to a different type of leadership, which became more firmly established during the course of the century. Now war was becoming an increasingly professional matter; this happened throughout Greece during the fourth century, and Athens was affected with the rest. The Peloponnesian war was evidently a crucial point in this evolution: the necessity of conducting long campaigns in increasingly remote areas induced the *strategoi* to have recourse, with even greater frequency, to the use of mercenary armies. And since mercenary service has always been a remedy for poverty, the destitution born from the ravages of war let loose on the road to the Aegean hordes of men ready to hire themselves out to the highest bidder.

Athens was for a long time unwilling to resort to mercenaries; but repeated defeats were to force her to accept this expedient. During the first years of the fourth century, it was with the aid of mercenaries that Iphikrates and Timotheos re-established Athenian positions in the Aegean and reopened the way through the Straits. Now mercenary warfare facilitated possible tactical innovations which were impossible for the heavily-armed hoplite forces. The mercenaries, with their lighter equipment, could form mobile groups capable of waging a guerrilla warfare that proved far deadlier to the enemy. Under such conditions, war became increasingly the business of professional soldiers. Thus certain *strategoi*, while retaining their functions in the magistracy, became increasingly prominent as generals. Such were Iphikrates, Timotheos, Chabrias and, later, Chares. True, ten *strategoi* were still appointed by election every year, and some of these were only incidentally soldiers. But the professional character of military life was becoming a fact that was patent to all. It was by no means peculiar to Athens; but the fact that Athens was affected by it shows the irreversible character of this development.

Its consequences in the political field were important. On the one hand the *strategos* who was in command of men whom he did not know, and for whom he was entirely responsible, acquired greater independence with respect to the city-state. On the other hand, a mercenary army was expensive; the city-state must therefore provide the *strategos* with the means to pay for it, for otherwise he would have to resort to expedients which did not always coincide with the interests of the state. During the early years of the fourth century such methods were in frequent use: plunder of the regions through which the army passed, excessive taxation exacted from allies, improvised customs duties imposed in the Straits. Sometimes more peaceful means were employed: Iphikrates praises the achievements of his mercenaries as farm labourers during the intervals between operations. Other *strategoi*, such as Timotheos, did not hesitate to mortgage their property to finance some expedition on which they were bent. It was safer, however, to get subsidies from the state. This required the *strategos* to come in person to justify 'his' war in front of the Assembly, or to find some orator who would defend his interests.[7]

At the same time as the *strategoi* became increasingly involved with military affairs, 'politics' became more and more the business of those professional politicians, the orators. Isokrates writes in the speech *On the Peace*:

> So far are we different from our ancestors that whereas they chose the same men to preside over the city and to be generals in the field, since they believed that one who could give the best counsel on this platform would best take counsel with himself when alone, we ourselves do the very opposite; for the men whose counsels we follow in matters of the greatest importance—those we do not see fit to elect as our generals, as if distrusting their intelligence, but men whose counsel no one would seek either on his own business or on that of the state—these we send into the field with unlimited authority, as if expecting that they will be wiser abroad than at home and will find it easier to take counsel on questions pertaining to the Hellenes than on those which are proposed for consideration here (154–5).

It is important, of course, not to be too dogmatic; at any rate during the first half of the fourth century, influential orators such as Kallistratos and Aristophon were *strategoi*, the former on two occasions, in 378–7 and in 373–2, the latter in 363–2. Their influence, however, was by no means limited to that relatively brief period of their political careers when they held office; and the phenomenon became more marked during the second half of the century—neither Demosthenes nor Aeschines were ever *strategoi*.

This professionalization of political life was reflected not only in the 'division of labour between orators and *strategoi*' (to quote A. Aymard) but also in the appearance of specialized posts within the magistracy, pre-eminently those concerned with finance. Expenses, indeed, had increased at the very time when the traditional resources associated with the exploitation of the empire were dwindling. Chiefly, this increase in expenses was due to the new needs of war. Money was required to pay the mercenaries, and moreover the rich were making ever greater efforts to escape from the burden of the trierarchies. Hence the necessity of procuring regular resources in order to avoid the extortionate methods we have already mentioned.

Two men were to endeavour to solve this difficult problem: Kallistratos, who dominated Athenian political life between 379 and 362/1 B.C., and Euboulos, whose influence began to be felt after 357. About 378 the former attempted a reform of the *eisphora*, the property-tax, intended to ensure its regular levying and an equitable distribution of the burden. The essence of his reform consisted in dividing the body of tax-payers into a hundred groups, each of which would represent the same fraction of taxable capital and comprise an equal number of citizens. It is hard to say whether the *eisphora* became, at the same time, a progressive tax, for there is much obscurity about the provisions of the law instituting the taxation-groups and many factors remain uncertain.[8] It may be doubted, in any case, whether the system was very effective: the *strategoi* maintained their exactions, and the difficulties confronting Athens were palliated only by recourse to the tributes exacted from the allies. In 362 the system was completed by the institution of the *proeisphora*. Henceforward the three hundred richest Athenians, evenly divided into groups (known as *symmoriai*), would advance the *eisphora* to the state, reimbursing themselves subsequently at the expense of the other tax-payers. The *proeisphora* was not established without a struggle. The rich, on whom the whole burden fell, complained, and the delay in collecting the taxes obliged the city-state to have recourse to methods which aroused fresh discontent, as we see from the earliest political speeches of Demosthenes. The institution of the *proeisphora* coincided roughly with the condemnation and exile of Kallistratos; that of the trierarchical taxation-groups in 357 heralds Euboulos' assumption of leadership in the city-state. It was in fact a friend of his, Periander, who proposed extending the system of taxation-groups to the trierarchy. The latter then ceased to be an individual liturgy and became a tax assumed collectively by the wealthiest citizens, grouped in twenty trierarchical *symmoriai*. The 'government' of Euboulos was to be distinguished, as we shall show later, by a resolutely pacifist foreign policy and at the same time by an undeniable economic recovery at home.

Now it was in his capacity as official in charge of the *theorika*, a post which he held uninterruptedly from 355 to 344, that he was able to direct the life of the *polis*. A relatively unimportant function thus became the springboard for important political activity.

It was only after Chaeronaea that the increased importance of financial offices eventually resulted in the creation of a magistrate's office which foreshadows that of the financial officials of the Hellenistic kings, the post of treasurer of the *dioikesis*, which was conferred on Lykourgos. This was the culmination of an evolution which definitely confirmed the separation of civil and military functions, together with the increasingly clear-cut specialization of both sorts.

Now this professionalization of political life, while corresponding to obvious technical needs, also implied a relative decrease in the political power of the *demos*. True, the latter still claimed to impose its control. But whereas formerly its decisions had been taken after careful consideration, now a passing enthusiasm for some individual would lead it to take contradictory measures, repudiating one day what had been decided the day before.

'The decrees of the Assembly', says Aristophanes' heroine in the *Ekklesiazusae*, 'are like those of drunken men, marked with madness' (ll. 137–9). Isokrates echoes him nearly half a century later in his speech *On the Peace*:

> We are versed beyond all others in discourse and in the conduct of affairs, but we are so devoid of reason that we do not hold the same views about the same question on the same day; on the contrary, the things which we condemn before we enter the assembly are the very things which we vote for when we are in session, and again a little later when we depart to our homes we disapprove of the things which we resolved upon here (52).

The many legal actions brought against *strategoi* and politicians during the first decades of the fourth century tell us clearly enough that the criticisms of Aristophanes and Isokrates were not dictated merely by a certain hostility to the regime, but that they reflected a state of affairs that undoubtedly existed.

Must we conclude, as does R. Sealey in his article on Kallistratos,[9] that Athenian political life in the fourth century consisted merely of conflicts between factions, each of which comprised men—orators and *strategoi*—united by their common local origin, by bonds of family or friendship, or by mere chance, and involving no political choice or the clash of antagonistic interests? This is perhaps a somewhat hasty judgment, and without denying the value of Sealey's arguments one is tempted to enquire whether other rifts are not perceptible.

We began by observing that for the writers of antiquity the fundamental antagonism in Greek city-states in the fourth century was that between the mass of the poor and the rich minority. Is it not possible to find traces of that antagonism in the political conflicts in Athens during the first half of the fourth century? Note first a comment by Aristophanes in the *Ekklesiazusae*: 'Must the ships be launched? [for a military expedition] The poor say yes, but the rich and the farmers say no' (ll. 197–8). This play was performed in 392 B.C. In the same year Sparta proposed peace conditions that were relatively favourable to Athens, since she authorized the Athenians to rebuild their long walls. According to Andokides, an orator persuaded the Athenians to reject the peace proposal by pointing out that the walls would not provide them with anything to eat.[10]

During the first years of the fourth century, then, there undoubtedly existed in the city-state a clear opposition between those who dreamed of revenge and those who were ready to accept an alliance with Sparta, provided it guaranteed freedom for the Athenians to manoeuvre in the Aegean. The former category clearly included the poor, particularly the urban *demos*, for whom war meant a secure wage, booty and the certainty of regular provisions; and also certain military leaders who flourished on profitable expeditions and personal glory, such as the *strategos* Aristophanes, of whom we learn in a speech by Lysias, a friend of Konon's who made a quick fortune in his wake. On the other side we find the peasantry, weary of endless wars and anxious to return to normal life in the countryside, as well as the bulk of the rich who dreaded the burden of trierarchies and property-taxes. Both parties, however, were equally desirous of restoring the hegemony of Athens in the Aegean and of ensuring the city's supplies, and there is no doubt that when the second maritime confederation was established, the great majority of the Athenians approved of it in principle. The anxiety to placate the allies and the King which finds expression in the decree of Aristoteles clearly reflects the consensus of opinion which had been achieved within the city-state, and if some people still yearned for an alliance with Sparta they seem to have had no opportunity of expressing it.

Things were to change after 371. The dwindling power of Sparta, increased difficulties in the Aegean, and Theban claims to hegemony, were once again to split Athenian opinion. For some Athenians, particularly for the rich, the imperialist solution was seen as pointlessly costly to an ever greater extent, and now that Sparta seemed no longer formidable they favoured a policy of *rapprochement* with the Peloponnesian state which implied giving up control of the sea and a certain hostility towards that now dangerous neighbour, Thebes. Kallistratos, who had been the contriver of the second maritime confederation, endeavoured to secure the triumph of this point of view during the years following the peace of 371 and the Spartan defeat at Leuktra. But the mass of the *demos* did not intend to renounce the advantages of an imperialist policy and was prepared to follow those who, out of interest or out of conviction, sought to maintain hegemony at any price. These could always resort to the armoury of traditional anti-Spartan propaganda to denounce their adversaries and offer the alternative of an alliance with Thebes, where a democratic regime had been in force since 379. The trial and condemnation of Kallistratos in 362 also coincided with the creation of the *proeisphora*, the result of which had been to put upon the rich the burden of the property-tax and the expense of military functions. Nor was it by chance that the period 362–357 witnessed the increase of extortionate demands on the allies and the establishment of new cleruchies. One has the impression that political conflicts in Athens had reached critical heights; scarcely a year passed without the *strategoi* in office being brought to trial. Partisans and adversaries of the imperialist policy clashed violently, while difficulties of provisioning worsened, forcing both sides to accept the principle of expeditions intended to secure the safe conduct of convoys of wheat.

Were there threats of more serious disturbance? The question is suggested by a reading of the clauses of the treaty of alliance which was concluded, shortly after the fall of Kallistratos, between Athens and a certain number of Peloponnesian states.[11] It was laid down here that the allies would undertake to intervene against anyone attempting to overthrow democracy in Athens in order to establish tyranny or oligarchy there. The author of the decree ratifying this alliance was that same Periander who, a few years later, successfully put through a law establishing trierarchical groups, which was indubitably inspired by the richer Athenian citizens. He belonged to that group of friends of Eubulos which, after the grave setback which the war against the allies constituted for the imperialist party, was to assume the leadership of the state. It is undeniable that these men, who for some years were to impose a policy of peace, had the support of the rich, of all those who bore the weight of the property-taxes and the trierarchies. The policy they sought to pursue is

31

expounded by Isokrates in the speech *On the Peace* and by Xenophon in *Ways and Means*: the renunciation of hegemony and imperialism, the exploitation of the resources of Attica and a policy calculated to attract foreigners and traders there. Such a policy was in opposition to all that had been attempted during the preceding years. It took account of the new balance which had been established in the Greek world since Sparta ceased to play an active part in the Aegean. But although it was to prove rewarding on the economic plane in the immediate future, it meant a renunciation by Athens of her role in the Aegean, and on this point it marked a rupture the importance of which must now be assessed.

The revival of Athenian imperialism

In the preceding pages we have attempted to show the new conditions of political life in Athens during the first half of the fourth century, and to disclose the antagonisms which, in the political field, reflected the break-up of the civic community. We have seen that these antagonisms, going beyond mere factional differences, brought rich and poor into conflict in the vital field of foreign policy. It is time now to retrace our steps and follow the evolution of that policy during the first decades of the fourth century.

In 404 B.C. Athens, defeated, had been forced to surrender her fleet, to destroy her walls and to renounce her external possessions. It is unlikely that the Athenian cleruchs of Lemnos, Imbros and Skyros returned to Attica; meanwhile all links between them and the metropolis were broken. As for Athens' former allies, they had been obliged, willingly or unwillingly, to join the Peloponnesian League. Athens herself had sworn to have the same friends and enemies as Sparta, and in the first years that followed her defeat, even after the restoration of the democracy, she fulfilled her obligations, albeit somewhat reluctantly.

Sparta's victory, however, and the establishment of Lacedaemonian harmosts in the Aegean islands, were to have unexpected results. Later, Athenian writers such as Isokrates were to explain Spartan policy in the early years of the century by the *hybris* fatal to victors. Actually, the war had had various repercussions on the Spartan state, which were to yield their full effect at the end of the century; but already their first symptoms were perceptible: Lysander's policy, the hostility between Lysander and Pausanias which was to reveal itself with particular acuteness during the period of the Thirty Tyrants, and the difficulties of Pausanias during the ensuing years. Sparta, having become against her will and in contradiction with her traditions a sea power, was now obliged almost involuntarily to adopt Athenian policy on her own account, even if only in the field of propaganda. If we add to this the crisis then being experienced by the Achaemenid empire, we find it easier to understand the campaigns which Agesilaus was to wage in Asia. That policy disturbed Artaxerxes, who had not forgotten the way Sparta had actively supported his brother Cyrus. Naturally, he would favour the ventures of those who attempted to oppose the king of Sparta, among them the Athenian Konon, friend of Evagoras, the ruler of Cyprus.

Konon had been in command of the Athenian fleet at Aigospotamoi, and he took good care not to return to Athens after that defeat, knowing only too well what fate awaited him. He had taken refuge with Evagoras and joined his service. In 397 we find him at the head of a detachment of forty Persian ships off the Carian coast, prepared to oppose the Spartan Derkyllidas. In 395 he was commander-in-chief of the Persian fleet, and the following year won the naval victory of Kneidos over the Spartan Peisander. This was to be followed by the expulsion of the Lacedaemonian garrisons, first from the Eastern Aegean and then from the islands. Konon succeeded in persuading the satrap Pharnabazos, who accompanied him on this expedition, to let him return to Athens: this would be the best way to be revenged on the Lacedaemonians. Xenophon, who reports these facts in the *Hellenica*, adds: 'Pharnabazos eagerly dispatched him to Athens and gave him additional money for the rebuilding of the walls. Upon his arrival Konon erected a large part of the wall, giving his own crews for the work, paying the wages of carpenters and masons, and meeting whatever other expense was necessary' (IV, viii, 9). It was thus thanks primarily to Persian money that the Athenians were able to rebuild their walls and, at least partially, to recover their authority in the Aegean.

The rupture between Sparta and her former allies, and the so-called Corinthian war which followed that rupture, enabled the Athenians to break off an alliance which had been forced upon them. When a *rapprochement* was initiated between Sparta and the Great King, Athens had sufficiently reconstituted her war material to be able to maintain her impetus. Thus in 389–388 Thrasyboulos, with a

33

fleet of forty ships, left for a cruise round the Hellespont, reintroduced the levying of taxes in the Bosphoros by gaining control of Byzantium, where he set up a democratic regime, and drove the Lacedaemonian garrisons from the cities of the island of Lesbos; he would perhaps have succeeded in regaining Rhodes from the Lacedaemonian party, had he not been killed in an ambush near Abydos. The following year, the Athenians sent Iphikrates into the Hellespont at the head of an army of 1,200 light troops with which, through a series of lucky strokes, he prevented the Spartan Anaxibios from regaining a foothold in that part of the Aegean world. The Athenians thus appeared to have recovered mastery of the Hellespont. They were once again installed in the Chersonese and in the islands, and the Spartan position seemed increasingly endangered.

Was this what gave rise to the *rapprochement* between the King and Sparta? We need to know more about the history of the Persian Empire to answer this question. We need, too, to take into account the intrigues of the various satraps, the recall of Konon's friend Pharnabazos, and the friendship between the satraps Ariobarzanes and Tiribarzes and the Spartan Antalkidas. In any case, the King's Peace in 386 brought a halt to Athenian ambitions in the Aegean. There was no longer any question of liberating the Greeks of Asia, nor of reconstituting an Athenian confederation. True, the Great King recognized Athenian possession of the islands of Lemnos, Imbros and Skyros, all comprising cleruchies. But any attempt to go beyond this would have invited intervention by the King's armies.

During the years that followed the King's Peace, however, Athens was to witness the development of a trend favourable to a revival of Athenian imperialism, but of an imperialism which would avoid the mistakes of the past. The King's Peace had been resented as an insult, and while never openly envisaging its repudiation but rather making a point of respecting it, Athenian propaganda sought to revive among the Greeks a sense of their common origin, their need to unite against the barbarian world as in the days of Xerxes, and the impossibility, in this connection, of trusting Sparta, which needed the help and subsidies of the Great King to assert its power. Isokrates' *Panegyricus* is undoubtedly the clearest expression of this propaganda. Years later, summing up the content of this speech, Isokrates recalled that it had been written 'at the time when the Lacedaemonians were the first power in Hellas, while our fortunes were at low ebb. In it I summon the Hellenes to make an expedition against the barbarians, and I dispute the right of the Lacedaemonians to take the lead' (*Antidosis*, 57).

In fact in this speech, composed in 380, that is to say six years after the King's Peace, Isokrates had applied himself to justifying the hegemony of Athens, with arguments drawn not only from the mythical past of the city (Demeter's gift of corn) but also from its less remote past (the role of Athens in the colonization of Ionia or in the Persian wars) and lastly from contemporary reality. Thus the commercial role of the Piraeus was explained by the concern of the Athenians to ensure subsistence for all Greeks:

> Since the different populations did not in any case possess a country that was self-sufficing, each lacking in some things and producing others in excess of their needs, and since they were greatly at a loss where they should dispose of their surplus and whence they should import what they lacked, in these difficulties also our city came to the rescue; for she established the Piraeus as a market in the centre of Hellas—a market of such abundance that the articles which it is difficult to get, one here, one there, from the rest of the world, all these it is easy to procure from Athens (*Panegyricus*, 42).

Moreover the intellectual and artistic superiority of Athens became an argument in favour of her hegemony over the Greek world:

> She affords the most numerous and the most admirable spectacles, some passing all bounds in outlay of money, some highly reputed for their artistic worth, and others excelling in both these regards; and the multitude of people who visit us is so great that, whatever advantage there is in our associating together, this also has been compassed by our city, Athens (ibid. 45).

And Isokrates concludes with the famous formula echoed from Thucydides:

> So far has our city distanced the rest of mankind in thought and in speech that her pupils have become the teachers of the rest of the world; and she has brought it about that the name 'Hellenes' suggests no longer a race but an intelligence, and that the title 'Hellenes' is applied rather to those who share our culture than to those who share a common blood (ibid. 50).

But Isokrates did not confine himself to justifying Athenian hegemony by theoretical reasons. He did not hesitate to glorify the

35

domination exercised by Athens over the Greeks in the preceding century:

> Up to this point I am sure that all men would acknowledge that our city has been the author of the greatest number of blessings and that she should in fairness be entitled to the hegemony. But from this point on, some take us to task, urging that after we succeeded to the sovereignty of the sea we brought many evils upon the Hellenes (ibid. 100).

He goes on to refute the arguments of the opponents of Athenian hegemony: if Athens sometimes acted harshly (as against the people of Melos or Skione) it was against people who deserved such treatment. To others, on the contrary, she displayed the greatest generosity, upholding the people against oligarchs and tyrants, defending those who trusted her against their enemies. Besides, if the Athenians did have any cause to reproach themselves, what about the Spartans? 'The severities under our administration could have been readily brought to an end by a single vote of the people, while the murders and acts of violence under their regime are beyond any power to remedy' (ibid. 114). Even more than the harshness of the Spartans' rule, it was the fact that this was exercised through the support of the Great King that made them reprehensible; when Athens lost her hegemony, the situation in Greece began to deteriorate:

> After the disaster which befell us in the Hellespont, when our rivals took our place as leaders, the barbarians won a naval victory, became rulers of the sea, occupied most of the islands, made a landing in Laconia, took Cythera by storm, and sailed round the whole Peloponnese inflicting damage as they went. . . . In those days we were constantly setting limits to the empire of the King, levying tribute on some of his subjects, and barring him from the sea; now, however, it is he who controls the destinies of the Hellenes, who dictates what they must each do, and who all but sets up his viceroys in their cities (ibid. 119–20).

There can be no doubt that in writing thus Isokrates was expressing not only his own opinion but that of a whole group of men close to him, among whom must be included Kallistratos and Timotheos, son of Konon. For these men the restoration of Athenian hegemony seemed an obvious necessity. It was indeed indispensable for the maintenance of internal peace and the provisioning of the city. They still recalled the grave difficulties endured by Athens, first in 404 and then in 388/7, when the Lacedaemonians had held up the convoys of grain. These men, moreover, were convinced of the greatness of Athens and of her leading place in the Greek world. Some of them, Timotheos for instance, may also have hoped to acquire certain glory and material advantages from a return to a policy of expansion in the Aegean. But they undoubtedly had behind them the great majority of Athenian public opinion, for reasons which have already been mentioned. Considering further that in the years that followed the King's Peace Spartan policy in the Peloponnese and in central Greece was to arouse much discontent, we can understand how Athens had no difficulty in convincing the Greeks of the necessity of an alliance of which she would be at the centre.

The second maritime confederation, preceded by bilateral alliances with the cities of the island of Lesbos, with Chios and with Byzantium, took definite shape in the decree of Aristoteles, the text of which has been preserved almost in its entirety.[12] This decree instituted an alliance between Athens and those of the Greek states which had sent delegates to a conference held in Athens during the winter of 378/7. A certain number of principles were laid down right at the start, which reflect the concern of the authors of the decree to avoid a repetition of the mistakes which, in the preceding century, had proved so disastrous to Athens. Thus the Athenians undertook to respect the autonomy and liberty of their allies, which meant that these would not have garrisons or governors imposed upon them, that they would be able to keep their constitutions and their laws even if these differed from the constitution and laws of Athens, and finally, most important, that they would not be forced to pay tribute. Moreover, no Athenian would be entitled on any pretext to own land or a house in allied territory.

The decree of Aristoteles does not give many precise details on the way the alliance functioned; but other texts allow us to fill in the gaps. The supreme authority was to be vested in the *synedrion* of the allies, composed of delegates from cities allied with Athens. The *synedrion*, whose seat was in Athens, would be consulted each time a decision involving the whole body of the allies was taken: thus Athens could no longer decide by herself on matters of common policy.

The object of the alliance being to maintain peace in the Aegean

37

by opposing acts of aggression by the Lacedaemonians, each member state had to participate in the defence of the whole group by sending contingents of men and by financial levies which, to begin with at any rate, had not the permanent and therefore humiliating character of the *phoros*. In case of disagreement it was the *synedrion*, sitting as a high court of justice, which had to decide. In particular, the *synedroi* would hear complaints in the case of breaches of the common pact by Athenian citizens.[13]

These undertakings, as well as the reference to the King's Peace in Aristoteles' decree, show clearly that the initiators of the second maritime confederation had no intention of merely reverting to the imperialism of the preceding century. It was necessary to consider the susceptibilities of the King, who might at any moment intervene on the side of the Lacedaemonians and jeopardize Athenian food supplies by some hostile action, and furthermore the susceptibilities of the Greeks, who were always liable to shift over to the Spartan side. In fact, during the first years that followed the constitution of the second confederation, particularly while Kallistratos exercised a preponderating influence on the politics of the city-state, it seems that Athens respected her undertakings. Until the conclusion of the peace of 371, the Athenians confined themselves to ensuring their supplies by keeping control over the Straits, their main efforts being concentrated in the Adriatic, where battles took place around Corcyra. The conclusion in 371 of a general peace, which renewed the King's Peace and brought a definite end to the war between Athens and Sparta, appeared moreover to realize the programme put forward by Isokrates in the *Panegyricus*, and the words attributed to Kallistratos by Xenophon in the *Hellenica* (VI, iii, 10 ff.) echo the proposals of the Athenian orator.

In fact, however, the earliest infringements of the confederation's pact date precisely from the time of that peace. General peace was only an empty word so long as Thebes refused to associate herself with it; and the problem for Athens was to know whether, faced with the Theban menace, she should take Sparta's side or maintain a prudent neutrality. In the former case she risked alienating a section of the allies, whose hostility towards Sparta had not decreased; in the second case, she might seem to be merely following in the wake of Thebes, and the war with Sparta might break out again at any moment. The Athenians appear to have pursued a wait-and-see policy to begin with. When, after Leuktra, a Spartan army under

Archidamos had been sent into Boiotia, and a Theban embassy came to demand help from Athens, it seems to have had a cool reception (*Hellenica*, VI, iv, 20). Athens, however, avoided taking sides and invited all the Greeks to renew the King's Peace; but when, two years later, the Thebans invaded Lakonia and threatened Sparta, and the Spartans turned to Athens for help, Athenian hostility towards Thebes was more openly displayed. However, according to Xenophon, Athenian opinion was still divided. When Spartan delegates recalled the common victories won of old, some of their hearers replied: 'That's what they say today, but when things were going well for them they made war against us' (ibid. VI, v, 35). The Athenians were more influenced by the speeches of the delegates from Corinth and Phlious. However, they were by no means unanimous, and it needed the eloquence of Kallistratos to bring about a decision (pseudo-Demosthenes LIX, 27); a relief expedition was sent out under Iphikrates.

The following year, when the problem of an alliance with Sparta was once more put before the Assembly, it was seen that the opponents of that alliance were still resolute, and were seizing every occasion—in this case the problem of leadership—to call it in question again. Athens, however, sent fresh reinforcements to the Peloponnese; but when in 367 a meeting of delegates from Greek city-states was held at Susa, one of the Athenian delegates, Timagoras, openly espoused the Theban side, as a result of which on his return he was sentenced to death. Those who favoured friendship with Thebes, or rather hostility towards Sparta, were still unyielding, however, and they succeeded in imposing the policy of alliance with the Arcadians, who were hostile to Sparta and had revived their confederation against that state, but who were also increasingly anxious to shake off the yoke of the Theban alliance. The opponents of Sparta scored a further point when the Corinthians sent back the Athenian garrisons established in their territory since 369 and initiated a *rapprochement* with Thebes in 365. In point of fact, during the ensuing period the Athenians seem to have disinvolved themselves from the affairs of the Peloponnese, and it was only after a fresh invasion of the Peloponnese by Epaminondas, when the Arcadian league had demanded help from Athenians and Spartans, that they once again fought side by side at the battle of Mantinea in 361. This battle, although its outcome was uncertain, sealed the decline of Sparta irrevocably, since the peace treaty which followed it, and to which the Athenians adhered, recognized the independence of Messenia.

Shortly before peace was concluded, Kallistratos had been definitely removed from power and driven into exile. With him, those who favoured a moderate imperialism and were willing to share influence with Sparta lost their authority, and in the years following Mantinea we find Athenian *strategoi* imperceptibly reverting to the practices which had led the empire to its downfall: the re-establishment of cleruchies at Potidaia in 362, and at Samos in 361, and the imposition of harsher taxation on the allies, these decisions being taken by the Assembly without consultation with the *synedrion*.[14] Analysing this period, Isokrates could write in 356:

> We think that, if we sail the sea with many triremes and compel the various states to pay contributions and send representatives to Athens, we have accomplished something to the purpose. But in fact we have been completely misled as to the truth; for of the hopes which we cherished not one has been fulfilled; on the contrary, we have reaped from them hatreds and wars and great expense (*On the Peace*, 29);

and further on:

> . . . we have reached such a degree of imbecility that, although we are ourselves in need of the necessities of daily existence, we have undertaken to support mercenary troops and we do violence to our own allies and extort money from them in order to provide pay for the common enemies of all mankind (ibid. 46).

Athens must renounce control of the sea:

> For it is this which plunged us into our present state of disorder, which overthrew that democratic government under which our ancestors lived and were the happiest of the Hellenes, and which is the cause, one might almost say, of all the ills which we both suffer ourselves and inflict upon the rest of the Hellenes. . . . For when with the help of ten thousand talents we were not able to retain it, how can we acquire it in our present state of poverty, especially when we are now addicted, not to the ways of life by which we gained it, but to those by which we lost it? (ibid. 64, 69).

For lack of resources, Athens could not lay claim to control of the

Plate 3 Athens, the Olympeion columns from the east. In the background the Acropolis

Plate 4 Athens, the Roman Agora and the Tower of the Winds

sea, and to those who replied that control of the sea was a means of procuring resources Isokrates retorted:

> [The war] has made us poorer; it has compelled many of us to endure perils; it has given us a bad name among the Hellenes; and it has in every way overwhelmed us with misfortune. But if we make peace and demean ourselves as our common covenants command us to do, then we shall dwell in our city in great security, delivered from wars and perils and the turmoil in which we are now involved amongst ourselves, and we shall advance day by day in prosperity, relieved of paying war-taxes, of fitting our triremes, and of discharging the other burdens which are imposed by war, without fear cultivating our lands and sailing the seas and engaging in those other occupations which now, because of the war, have entirely come to an end. Nay, we shall see our city enjoying twice the revenues which she now receives, and thronged with merchants and foreigners and resident aliens, by whom she is now deserted (ibid. 19, 21).

Isokrates wrote thus at the moment when Athens was in the throes of her war against the allies, which was in fact a revolt by a section of the Aegean allies. This had started the previous year, in 357, with the defection of the larger islands which, since 378, had been allied with Athens. Was this secession perhaps the result of intrigues by the Charian dynast, Mausolos? In any case, Rhodes, Chios and Kos, backed by their ally, Byzantium, were, at the beginning of summer 357, the scene of oligarchic revolutions, which were promptly followed by a withdrawal from the Athenian alliance. Chares, at the head of a corps of mercenaries, immediately came to block Chios. But the fleet, under Chabrias, suffered a severe defeat in midsummer. Chares then returned towards the Hellespont and undertook operations against Byzantium, from the Thracian Chersonese.

The following year the allied fleet attacked and devastated the Athenian cleruchies of Lemnos and Imbros, and then threatened Samos, where it met with opposition from Athenian cleruchs. Early that summer a supplementary fleet of sixty ships commanded by Timotheos and Iphikrates came to join Chares' fleet, and the famous battle of Embata took place off Chios in the autumn of 356, following which Chares, who had joined battle alone and been defeated, brought a lawsuit against Iphikrates and Timotheos. The war lasted one year longer, and was notable essentially for the operations undertaken by Chares in Asia. But in the end, Athens, driven to the wall by an ultimatum from the Great King, was forced to yield and make peace with her adversaries, recognizing their independence.

The conclusion of peace was no doubt connected with a change in the ruling personnel of the city-state. Since 357, indeed, the friends of Euboulos seemed to be yielding to the extreme imperialists, whose policy was both inspired and carried out by Chares. Already in 357, as we have seen, Periander, by instituting trierarchical groups, had spread the burden of the trierarchies so as to diminish each individual's share of the duty. The following year Euboulos had become president of the officers in charge of the theoric fund. One inevitably draws the conclusion that the peace of 355 represented a repudiation of the policy that had been followed by Chares for the past two years, and consequently implied a move towards a new policy.[15]

As we have seen, Isokrates in his speech *On the Peace* had traced the broad lines of that policy: peace abroad, and at home a development of the resources of Attica in order, more particularly, to revive the commercial activity of the Piraeus. That same year Xenophon, whose connections with the Euboulos group were well known, published his *Ways and Means*. The same aim was expressed here, but the author dwelt at greater length on the measures needed to set the Athenian economy on its feet again. Before discussing these it is necessary to recall briefly what the economic activity of Athens had been during the first half of the fourth century.

The revival of economic activity

We have already seen that the years following the Peloponnesian war had been difficult ones for Athens. The flight of twenty thousand slaves at the time of the occupation of Dekeleia by the Spartans had disorganized the artisan class; the war and then the tyranny of the Thirty had driven from the Piraeus the foreign traders who used to sojourn there, and finally the raids by Lacedaemonians, particularly during the last years of the war, had been very savage and had devastated the Attic countryside.

The opening years of the fourth century had witnessed no perceptible improvement. The problem of supplies, in particular, remained acute, and the action brought by Lysias against the grain merchants reveals the gravity of the situation at the beginning of the eighties, as well as the measures taken by the Athenian state to prevent hoarding and speculation. As we have seen, the *Ploutos* of Aristophanes describes the distress of the peasantry in vivid terms.

It must be admitted, however, that Athens gradually succeeded in regaining a certain equilibrium, which the conclusion of the second naval confederation was obviously to strengthen. For a few years we hear no further mention of supply problems. The Athenians had regained their footing in the Straits and once more controlled the entry of grain. The fleet had been reconstituted, and this implied a renewal of activity in arsenals and ports. Furthermore, it seems that this period witnessed the beginning of a revival of mining.

To assess the scale of this we have a valuable source of information: the lists of concessionaries drawn up by the officials in charge of allocation. Moreover, Aristotle in the *Constitution of Athens* gives a description of the method of allocation of mining concessions which is certainly valid for the period at which he was writing, but which presumably corresponds to a reorganization undertaken in the seventies of the fourth century, and forming part of the general process of recovery for which Kallistratos was responsible.[16] Indeed, the oldest list that has come down to us dates from the year 367/6. Others follow, spaced out until the end of the century, the longest and most complete belonging to the period 350/338. Taking into account the inevitable gaps in our documentation, we can thus assume that the recovery connected with a new system of concessions was slow at first, since in 356 in *Ways and Means*, Xenophon still complained that most of the mines were inactive, and only got under way after 356, that is to say from the moment when Athens had to renounce large-scale imperialism in the Aegean and was obliged to turn her resources to the best possible account.

Aristotle's text distinguishes between two types of concession, the *ergasima*, mines that were working, and the *synkechoremena*, mines which had not yet been exploited or which had been abandoned a long time ago.[17] The former were conceded for a period of three years, the others for a longer period—seven or ten. The concession was granted on payment of a rent that seems very low, between 20 and 150 drachmas, with the exception of a few high prices which must refer to more important concessions (2,000 to 9,000 drachmas), so low in fact that some scholars have formed the unlikely conclusion that the rent was paid at each prytany.[18] More probably the rent was paid annually, or else a single sum was paid for the whole duration of the concession.

We cannot but be struck, on considering the officials' lists, by the fact that they bear the names of rich Athenians and even, frequently, of illustrious men who were at the same time landed proprietors and owned surface factories, and who moreover are known to have been trierarchs.[19] In some cases there was a family tradition, as for instance with Nikias and Nikeratos of Kydantidai, the grandson and greatgrandson of the fifth-century *strategos*, who had a thousand slaves working in the mines. In other cases a new activity seems to have been involved, and one may wonder what led rich Athenians to take up mining concessions. Undoubtedly the love of wealth, as the philosophers called it, had something to do with this phenomenon. In *Ways and Means* Xenophon comments, precisely with reference to the mines: 'No one ever yet possessed so much silver as to want no more; if a man finds himself with a huge amount of it, he takes as much pleasure in burying the surplus as in using it.' Later he specifies the various 'uses' to be made of it: 'The men will spend money on fine arms and good horses and magnificent houses and establishments, and the women go in for expensive clothes and gold jewellery.' In case of war or of bad harvest 'there is a much more insistent demand for cash to pay for food and mercenaries'.

Unquestionably this double aim may have been that of wealthy Athenians and leaders of the city-state. The example of Midias, rich adversary of Demosthenes, who owned a concession at Laurion, is highly significant in this respect, and undoubtedly the concessionaries referred to in a speech by Hypereides were also motivated by 'the love of wealth'. The growth of private luxury was a characteristic feature of Athenian life in the fourth century, and may have encouraged many rich Athenians to become concessionaries. It was moreover in the interest of the state for the exploitation of mines to revive, not so much because of the revenue directly derived from this—we have seen that the rent paid was relatively low—as because its prosperity depended on the income of rich individuals. This renders all the more astonishing the suggestion made by Xenophon in Chapter IV of *Ways and Means*. Here he expresses the wish to see the state replace individuals to some extent in two fields. On the one hand, as slave-owner. It is known, in fact, that the concessionaries of mines put slaves to work in those galleries which excavations have uncovered, in which labour must have been extremely arduous, considering the conditions of ventilation and the narrowness of the tunnels. The slaves might belong to the concessionary; but it seems that most frequently the concessionary hired them from a slave-owner at a rate of one obol per man per day. He thus avoided the expense of buying slaves; he merely had to feed them from day to day and to pay the owner his dues. As for the owner, he derived a clear profit from his slave-capital which, if the slave worked three hundred days a year, might be as advantageous as the interest on a shipping loan (a slave in the mines, in the fourth century, was worth some 300 drachmas). It was this system which Xenophon suggested the city-state should adopt:

> What may well excite surprise is that the state, being aware that many private individuals are making money out of her, does not imitate them . . . were my proposals adopted, the only innovation would be, that just as private individuals have built up a permanent income by becoming slave owners, so the state would become possessed of public slaves, until there were three for every citizen (*Ways and Means*, IV, 14).

Xenophon next expounds the steps to be taken in order for the state, putting up a relatively modest sum to begin with, to collect a first contingent of ten thousand slaves, who would bring in annually 100 talents—provided they worked every day of the year. To those who might object that these slaves might perhaps find no one to hire them, he replied with the second part of his plan: that the state itself should become a mine-owner.

> The Athenians . . . are divided into ten tribes. Now assume that the state were to offer each tribe an equal number of slaves, and that when new cuttings were made, the tribes were to pool their luck. The result would be that if one tribe found silver, the discovery would be profitable to all; and if two, three, four, or half the tribes found, the profits from these works would obviously be greater. Nothing that has happened in the past makes it probable that all would fail to find (ibid. IV, 30).

Xenophon further envisaged the possibility of similar co-operation between individuals, which would diminish the risks run by each separate prospector, and it is known that such associations were to be formed after 350. On the other hand no attempt was made to put into practice the project of large-scale purchase of slaves by the state, nor the exploitation of mines by the tribes. None the less, the interest displayed by the author of *Ways and Means* in mine-working certainly reflects the concern of the group of men who now took in hand the government of the city-state, and it was not by accident that a revival of mining activity took place during the following years.

In the same treatise Xenophon examines another aspect of the economic life of Athens, her commercial development. He dwells on

the unrivalled amenities and advantages of our city as a commercial centre. In the first place . . . she possesses the finest and safest accommodation for shipping, since vessels can anchor here and ride safe at their moorings in spite of bad weather. Moreover, at most other ports merchants are compelled to ship a return cargo because the local currency has no circulation in other states; but at Athens they have the opportunity of exchanging their cargo and exporting very many classes of goods that are in demand, or, if they do not want to ship a return cargo of goods, it is sound business to export silver; for, wherever they sell it, they are sure to make a profit on the capital invested (ibid. III, 2).

The Piraeus had played this commercial role since the fifth century, Thucydides having already ascribed similar proposals to Perikles in 431. The harbour, which had been built and equipped to shelter Athenian triremes, had quickly become an important agglomeration, following plans drawn up by Hippodamos of Miletos. Foreign traders thronged to it. Covered markets and shelters for ships had been built, and rich metics had their homes there; one such was the armourer Kephalos, father of Lysias, whose house was the scene of Plato's dialogue, the *Republic*. There were hostelries for transient foreigners, and a whole motley population of poor citizens, metics and slaves lived there. This was where Thrasyboulos had settled after the capture of Phyle, both in order to control the provisioning of the city and because he knew he would find many supporters there. There can be no doubt that the Piraeus was the democrats' strongest base of operations.

Had the port maintained its activity in the fourth century? Although in *Ways and Means* Xenophon considers measures likely to bring back traders in large numbers, it would perhaps be rash to conclude that these had deserted the port and that the commercial activity of Athens had declined. To be sure, as we have already seen, until 380 the difficulty of procuring grain supplies might suggest that the traders' activity had slowed down, or that those who had substantial cargoes were tempted to unload them elsewhere. However, it would be a mistake to overstress this point, or to exaggerate the effect of the policy of the Thirty towards the metics. Xenophon himself dwelt on the abundance and variety of goods to be found in the Piraeus. Undoubtedly the reopening of the Straits route from 378 onwards, the re-establishment of the cleruchies and the construction of ships to fulfil the needs of Athenian maritime policy must have restored to the Piraeus its former activity. Even the slowing-down of Athenian production cannot have had much effect on the volume of barter, in so far as that production played no great part in these exchanges, apart from money payments. The Piraeus was a convenient port of call for traders, and it is unlikely that they avoided it. Yet there are certain indications that they made a somewhat shorter stay there. There appears to have been a change, in the fourth century, in the status of the metics, who could now claim that title without definitely settling in the city.[20] Consequently, the population of the Piraeus, which consisted largely of foreigners, became more fluctuating, according to circumstances, and the revenue that the state derived from these foreigners became less constant. This would explain the measures recommended by Xenophon with regard to them: that the rulings of commercial courts should be made more expeditious, that aliens should be given easier access to these courts, provided with hostelries and covered markets, and welcomed with warmer hospitality, rewards and honours. We notice, in fact, that dating from the middle of the century the procedure of mercantile suits was speeded up, and that aliens began to enjoy the same privileges as citizens when they appeared before the commercial courts, now presided over by *thesmothetes*, instead of having to be represented by a 'patron'.[21] It is no less striking that the decrees conferring honours on aliens who had ensured Athens' vital supplies became more numerous after 360, while the granting of the privilege of *enktesis* became more general.[22]

The large number of civil lawsuits relating to commercial affairs included among the writings of Demosthenes reflects both the real activity of the commercial courts and also the development of 'business' in Athens during the second half of the fourth century. It was at this period that associations of a more or less temporary nature were formed between ship-owners and merchants, and that written contracts and banking activities became more widespread. Pasion, the famous banker of the first half of the century, was personally connected with Kallistratos. His wealth was considerable, consisting of credits, slaves and property reckoned at twenty talents. His son Apollodoros inherited his property and took up a political career. The bank passed to Phormion, his former slave, in whose hands it continued to prosper.

The business world which we discover through the works of Demosthenes was a remarkably mixed society. It included both citizens and aliens, the former generally providing the capital which enabled ship-owners and traders to undertake the ventures from which both hoped to profit. Pontus was frequently the object of such campaigns: in the cities of the kingdom of the Bosphoros where some of these traders had permanent agents, they bought grain primarily but also dried fish, slaves and ores, which were paid for in coin or with weapons or vases. It is in the Crimea that the largest number of the so-called Kertch vases have been discovered; their artistic value is considerably less than that of the large red-figure vases of the preceding century.

But the Pontic region was not the only one to be visited by traders from Athens; Egypt, Cyrenaica and, above all, the West were also connected with Athens by a whole network of trade. True, it would be absurd to imagine any regular system of exchanges, and the presence of Athenian mercenaries in Egypt or in Sicily is not enough to establish the existence of continuous commercial relations. Such relations did exist, however, and they brought the products of the whole Mediterranean basin pouring in to the Piraeus. Although pirates often hindered merchants in the pursuit of their trade, none the less trade was carried on and Athens remained the indisputable centre of it.

However, the city enjoyed only a limited part of its benefits: merely the levying of taxes on the merchandise that came in or went out, and a very modest annual tax on resident aliens (12 drachmas for a man, 6 for a woman). It is obviously almost impossible, for lack of figures, to estimate the amount of the revenue thus acquired; but it can scarcely have been sufficient to cover the ever-growing expenses that the state had to face. As for individual profits, most of them were made by aliens, resident or transient, and only rarely benefited the state. The metics were not subject to the trierarchy and were only called upon to serve in the hoplite infantry. Their contribution to the defence of the state was thus relatively modest, and they assumed only a partial share of public duties.

Thus the unquestioned prosperity of the Athenian economy in the fourth century could in no way solve the crisis that the city-state was undergoing. Increasingly, the real sources of wealth lay outside it. True, there were some citizens who had interests in commercial affairs, others who derived large profits from their mining concessions, and even, as we shall see later, landowners ready to take advantage of the difficulties of supply to speculate on the price of commodities in the market. These men, increasingly dominated by a love of money which tended to obliterate differences of origin, tended also to concern themselves less and less with the affairs of the state. One can assume that they supported the 'pacific' policy of Euboulos, in so far as it freed them from the burden of trierarchies and property taxes and allowed them to devote themselves more to their private interests. Furthermore, the decline in the power of Sparta and the withdrawal of Thebes after Mantinea justified a growing lack of interest in Aegean affairs. It was still necessary, however, to ensure the safety of supplies by retaining the islands where there were cleruchies and the Chersonese, and exercising more or less direct control over Thrace.

This security, since 359, had been threatened by the activities of a newcomer in the Aegean world, Philip, king of the Macedonians.

3   The conflict with Macedonia (359–337 B.C.)

From 359 onwards the dominant factor in the history of Athens is her conflict, at first indirect then increasingly overt, with the ruler of a barbarian kingdom lying on the borders of the Hellenic world: Philip of Macedonia.

Philip and Athens—the struggle between parties and the decay of political life

The kingdom of Macedonia in 359   Macedonia, lying to the north of Thessaly, had hitherto played only a secondary part in the affairs of the Aegean world. The Greeks regarded its inhabitants as barbarians. In fact, since the region had provided the passage for the successive invaders of the Balkan peninsula, the population of Macedonia was the result of a fusion of diverse elements, Illyrians, Thracians and Epirotes mingled with Achaeans; but very soon the kings of Macedonia had asserted their Hellenic origin, claiming descent from the kings of Argos. Very soon, too, they began to interfere in Greek affairs. It was primarily with Athens that they had to deal, because of the interest which that city had taken in the northern Aegean ever since the time of Peisistratos, who had himself maintained good relations with Amyntas I and had been allowed by that ruler to settle in Rhaikelos during his second exile. During the Persian wars, Macedonia was subjugated by the Great King, but it was Alexander I of Macedonia who, after Salamis, conveyed Mardonios' proposals to Athens. Relations grew somewhat strained during the years that followed. The establishment of Athenian colonies in Thrace aroused the concern of Alexander I, who may have been responsible for the massacre of Drabeskos. The foundation of Amphipolis was also resented as a direct threat to the kingdom. This explains the often hostile attitude of King Perdikkas II, who succeeded Alexander, particularly during the first years of the Peloponnesian war.

The authority of the throne was greatly strengthened by Archelaos, successor to Perdikkas II, in particular through the constitution of a substantial army which foreshadowed Philip's phalanx and through the construction of a network of fortresses which were to make Macedonia into an impregnable territory. Considered by Plato as a tyrant, Archelaos seems in fact to have played in Macedonia, during the closing years of the fifth century, a role analogous to that of the Greek tyrants of the sixth century, presumably reflecting considerable transformations in the social and political structure of his country. His death in 394 marked the beginning of a period of crisis which was to end in 359 with the accession of Philip.

The latter was the younger brother of King Perdikkas III, who had died leaving as heir his young son, Amyntas IV; Philip at first stood guardian to the child, but soon eliminated him and had himself proclaimed sole king. Master of Macedonia, he was to set himself a twofold aim: to strengthen the authority of the throne in his own country, and to make Macedon the arbiter of the Greek world.[1]

To achieve the first of these aims, Philip carried on the policies of Archelaos. He organized the phalanx which was to prove the essential instrument of his conquests. He undertook the systematic exploitation of the mines of Mount Pangaeus, so as to ensure the financial resources necessary for his major designs. Finally, in order to be able to turn his attention to the Aegean, he took care to hold in check within the country those regions which were not yet subject to the authority of the throne, and on its borders the neighbours who might still constitute some sort of threat, Illyrians, Epirotes or Thracians.

The conflict with Athens up to 340   As we have already seen, Athens was going through a particularly critical period when Philip acceded to the throne. Her difficulties in Euboea and her war against the allies prevented her from intervening when Philip succeeded, almost without striking a blow, in seizing Amphipolis, Pydna and Potidaia. On the collapse of the empire, after the war against the allies, the government of the city-state was taken over by men determined not to let themselves become involved in risky wars for the defence of an empire which was visibly disintegrating; this clearly encouraged

Philip's first enterprises. It took a direct threat to Thermopylai, with all the memories that this evoked, for Athens to bring herself to send troops to guard the pass; but during the next few years Philip was able to intervene freely in Thrace without arousing any significant reactions. It was not until he attacked Olynthos that an expeditionary force, equipped with limited weapons, was sent in response to the Olynthians' request. Olynthos eventually succumbed, however, and Philip was able to resume operations in Thessaly, destined to bring the sacred war to an end and to force the Phokians to accept peace, in which most of the Greek city-states joined in 346.

During the negotiations which then took place and which are known to us in detail through the speeches of Aeschines and Demosthenes on the *Embassy*, Philip took advantage of his adversaries' slowness to complete his conquest of Thessaly, decisively crushing the Phokians and, with the aid of the Thebans, gaining admission to the Amphiktyonic League at Delphi, and finally occupying Thrace, whose king, an ally of Athens, he had excluded from the negotiations. Peace was ratified none the less, making Philip, with the support of the Amphiktyonic League, the guarantor of the balance of power within the Greek world.[2]

This balance was to be maintained, not without difficulty, during the six years following the ratification of peace. While in Athens, as we shall see, the partisans and the adversaries of Philip were to mutually accuse one another of treachery, the King of Macedon strengthened his positions in the northern Aegean. In 345 he invaded Dardania, then Illyria, in order to ensure the safety of his western frontiers. In 344, in answer to an appeal from the people of Thessaly, he intervened in that country to expel the last tyrants who still held sway there. He next undertook the reorganization of the country, regrouping the cities into four districts and setting decadarchies at the head of them. He had himself, in 342 at the latest, been elected archon for life of the Thessalian League, and a Macedonian garrison had been established at Pheres.

During the winter of 343–342, Philip intervened in Epiros to restore the authority of Alexander the Molossian. This aroused anxiety in the Greek cities of Leukas and Ambrakia, and they appealed to their metropolis, Corinth, which requested the help of Athens. An expeditionary force was sent to Ambrakia, and Philip desisted. The result of Athens' prompt success was to secure for that city the favour of Peloponnesian states which hitherto had rejected her advances: Corinth, the Achaean League, the Arcadians, Argos and the Messenians drew closer to Athens.

This aroused Philip's anxiety, and he now attempted to win the goodwill of the Athenians by offering them the small island of Halonnese. On the rejection of his offer, following an appeal by the orator Hegesippos, he assumed a hostile attitude. Perhaps he may also have been disturbed at the attempted *rapprochement* between the Athenians and the Great King; the latter, in fact, after crushing a revolt in Phoenicia in 345 and reasserting his sway over Egypt in 343, was now attempting to restore Persian power in Asia and in particular to lay hands once more on the southern bank of the Straits, after capturing Hermias, tyrant of Atarneos and a personal friend of Philip's.

Philip, feeling his authority in Thrace threatened, therefore seized that part of the Odrysian kingdom that still remained independent, and forced the Greek cities of the Thracian coast and the Euxine to form an alliance with him, directly threatening the Athenian cleruchies of the Chersonese. The Athenians then sent an expedition led by the *strategos* Diopeithes, who, being short of resources, had recourse to extortions and threatened Cardia, an ally of Philip's. In spite of Cardia's protests, fresh reinforcements were sent to the *strategos* and alliances concluded with Byzantium, Abydos, Chios and Rhodes.

At the same time Athens sought a *rapprochement* with the Peloponnesian cities and re-established her authority over Euboea. In March 340 a congress of the allies of Athens was held, which adopted the principle of a general war against Philip. This was to break out a few months later, during the summer of 340. The policy which Demosthenes had been pressing so determinedly since his *First Philippic* in 351 was finally ratified by the Greeks as a body.

Party conflict and the decadence of political life in Athens from 355 to 340 Most of Demosthenes' great political speeches were composed and delivered between these two dates, except for the *Speech on the Crown*. These speeches clearly provide fascinating evidence about political life in Athens during those years, which were the closing years of her great history.

In 355, when he delivered his first political speech against Leptines and wrote those against Androtion and Timokrates for 'clients', Demosthenes seems not to have taken any very definite political position as yet. The son of a rich slave-owner who had made his money by manufacturing arms and furniture, he had lost the greater part of his fortune through the mismanagement of dishonest guardians, and this had obliged him while still young to take up the profession of advocate, that is, to compose speeches for Athenians involved in private or public lawsuits. The speech *Against Leptines* seems to have been the first that he delivered himself, in his own name, during a suit brought against one Leptines who, shortly after the Social War, in order to cope with the enormous financial problems then confronting Athens, had proposed a draft decree suppressing the immunities then enjoyed by a certain number of Athenians or aliens as benefactors to the city. Modern scholars fail to agree about the behaviour and opinions of the orator at the time of his first entry into political life.[3] Some have seen him at that time as a supporter of Euboulos, defender of the interests of the propertied classes who would suffer from the measures proposed by Leptines or by Androtion. Others, on the contrary, have tried to prove that from that moment Demosthenes had chosen the policy which he was to uphold during the ensuing years: the defence of Athenian liberty and democracy.[4]

This is not the real problem, however, and it is of little importance that Demosthenes, once a friend of Euboulos, should have broken with him later. The essential point is to ascertain the conflicting trends in Athenian public opinion following the collapse of the empire.

We have already seen how the rich, property-owning classes had for the most part abandoned an imperialist policy. Isokrates' speech *On the Peace* and Xenophon's *Ways and Means*, which appeared at the time of the first speeches of Demosthenes, clearly express their point of view. None the less, the men who governed the city-state were faced with a twofold problem: the all-important one of ensuring Athens' food supplies at all costs, and the problem of financial resources, since warships were needed to safeguard grain convoys. It was to make possible a fairer distribution of the burden of the trierarchy that Periander, a friend of Euboulos, had brought in the institution of trierarchical groupings which transformed the former liturgy into a tax affecting a larger number of Athenians. When, on the eve of Chaeronea, Demosthenes was to get the trierarchy re-established, he was to insist on the fact that Periander's law had been a means for the richer citizens to evade part of their obligations. The decrees proposed by Androtion and Leptines, claiming from tax-payers the arrears of their dues and suppressing immunities, seemed at first glance to be aimed at the same end, and it has been argued that they had been inspired by the friends of Euboulos. Things are not quite so simple, however; for this might have been a case of a demagogic bid for popularity, whose practical benefits would be negligible. That, at any rate, is what Demosthenes claims.[5] If in fact we are to admit that Euboulos' policy was essentially aimed at restoring the financial balance of Athens, such measures could only increase the discontent of those who would be its victims, without much real advantage to the state. Such victims would be, on the one hand, the mass of small tax-payers, on the other the 'benefactors' of Athens, whose goodwill was none the less increasingly necessary. Specious as are Demosthenes' arguments, particularly with respect to Leukon, the ruler of the Bosphoros, who would obviously not have been affected by the decree, the fact remains that the suppression of the immunities enjoyed by certain foreigners might drive them away from Athens at the very moment when efforts were being made to attract them thither, and conflicted directly with the measures recommended by Xenophon in his *Ways and Means*. It is thus indubitable that, by attacking these decrees, Demosthenes was defending the point of view of the supporters of Euboulos, yet it is not necessary to explain the fact by personal interests, such as the recovery of his fortune.

It is quite possible, however, that while making his political debut in the wake of Euboulos, he did not share all the latter's views. As has often been pointed out, he had been deeply influenced, like many of his contemporaries, by a reading of Thucydides. Because he was younger than most of the men in Euboulos' circle he may have believed that recovery was still possible. Moreover Isokrates, disillusioned though he was, shows in *On the Peace* that he had not quite given up hope of hegemony for Athens. He merely wished for it to be exercised by other means, and to be the result of the Greeks' spontaneous wish. As for the provisioning of Athens, this was considered a vital necessity by everyone; in particular one cannot fail to be impressed by the fact that in 353/2 there were 349 ships in dock in the Piraeus[6] and that the following year new cleruchs were sent to Samos.

It is certain, however, that if the 'pacifist' party enjoyed wide support from Athenian opinion at that time, that support was not unanimous. Certain ambitious *strategoi*, among whom Chares must certainly be included, had not given up hope of taking their revenge on the allies. Following the peace which was a denial of the whole policy he had been urging since 357, Chares had offered his services to the King; but he undoubtedly had friends in Athens, ready to defend a more energetic foreign policy and sure of the support of the urban *demos* to that end. In his speeches *Against Leptines* and *Against Timokrates*, Demosthenes refers to the dangers which once threatened the Athenian democracy and lavishes sarcasms on those who think that such threats are now averted.[7] Does this imply that a certain disquiet then prevailed in Athens, from which a would-be tyrant might profit? If the danger of oligarchy did in fact seem to be excluded, since no one now sought to challenge the regime, yet popular discontent might, here as elsewhere, lead to the seizure of power by an individual. A general whose prestige was as great as that of Chares unquestionably represented a threat. This notwithstanding, it is not certain that the men who in 355/4 proposed the demagogic measures opposed by Demosthenes were friends of Chares, nor even that they all sought the same goal. We cannot fail, however, to be impressed by the fact that Lepotines' law was defended by Aristophon of Azenia, whose close friendship with Chares had frequently been demonstrated, recently on the occasion of the lawsuit brought against Iphikrates and Timotheos after the battle of Embata. Aristophon, however, was an old man, whose influence was on the wane, while Androtion and Leptines were secondary figures of no great weight. The 'imperialist' party was therefore unlikely to win much support from the *demos*, and there seemed little hope for Chares of any strong foreign policy in the near future in which he could win distinction.

Things were to change after 353/2. It is of course difficult to say whether the volte-face of Demosthenes reflects an inordinate political ambition which could not find fulfilment in the shadow of Euboulos, or a clear apprehension of the danger represented by Philip. In any case, Philip was to become the main enemy in the orator's mind, and all the energies of the city-state must be used in the necessary struggle against him. Now it is quite clear that when he thus denounced the danger that Philip represented, Demosthenes had little chance of gaining a hearing in the late fifties of the fourth century. At that time, many people thought of Philip merely as one of those princelings of the northern Aegean whom Athens, of course, would like to include in her alliance, but who caused her far less anxiety than what was happening in Euboea or in the Peloponnese. The men around Euboulos, faithful to their choice of a resolutely pacifist policy, could justifiably consider that Philip's political activities were no concern of theirs. Certainly, when Philip approached Thermopylai, there was a reaction, but this was soon dropped when Macedonian pressure relaxed. We can obviously wonder if from that time onwards Philip sought to win over influential politicians to his cause, if the 'Macedonian' party was already in embryo on the eve of the first *Philippic*. It is not very easy to answer such a question, since we must obviously take Demosthenes' bias into account: many of those whom he was later to accuse of being in the service of Philip had as yet no relation with the Macedonian. It is, however, unquestionable that between 351 and 346 Philip's influence increased within the city-states of Greece, and that Athens was no exception to this general phenomenon.

It was in 346 that Isokrates wrote his *Philip*, that fictitious oration in which he decides to offer to the king of Macedonia the role he had vainly dreamed of seeing Athens play, that of leader of the Greek city-states, in an effort to put an end to their quarrels and unite them in the struggle against the hereditary enemy, the Asian barbarian, whose lands, once conquered, could be allocated to the needy horde of landless Greeks who constituted a threat to the peace of honest citizens.[8] This is a recurrent theme with the Athenian orator, who is known to have exerted a certain influence on those who had been his pupils, and whose *On the Peace* (356 B.C.) expressed, clearly enough, the broad lines of the programme to be followed by Euboulos in the years to come. Does this imply that Euboulos and his circle shared the views of Isokrates and, seeing Philip as the future leader of Greece, set the aims pursued by the latter above the interests of Athens? This is unlikely: they were rational politicians, they could not disregard the need for provisioning Athens, and as we have already seen, they did not neglect the defence of the Straits. On the other hand, they may have been less alarmed than was Demosthenes by Philip's manoeuvres in northern Greece. Although, for the reasons already suggested, they were certainly pacifists, having opted for neutrality and seeking to maintain their city-state in that position, they were not necessarily supporters of the Macedonian.

Others, however, might have gone farther and openly wished for an increase in Philip's power. Their motives are certainly open to question. Some of them, undoubtedly, as was to become increasingly clear after 346, received direct encouragement and substantial subsidies from Philip. The existence of Philip's agents in Athens is not merely a figment of Demosthenes' imagination, even if some distinction must be made between the obscure figures cited by the orator and his leading adversary, Aeschines. Others may have chosen Philip's side for different reasons, which it may be interesting to examine. In a speech delivered a few years after Chaironea, the orator Hypereides, one of the leaders of the anti-Macedonian party, accused his opponents of being enemies of democracy and heirs to those who formerly admired Sparta.[9] This fits in with certain accusations uttered by Demosthenes against Philip, namely that he was primarily the enemy of the Athenian constitution.[10] If we accept his accusations as being well founded, the 'Macedonian' party appears as the latest incarnation of the former 'oligarchic' party.

What arguments are there to bear out this thesis, apart from the biased assertions of Hypereides and Demosthenes? For the period before Chaironea, we have practically no proof of any connection between the oligarchy and the partisans of Philip. We have already seen that, after the restoration of the democracy in 403, there was no longer any oligarchic party in Athens, and that at no time during the fourth century do we witness any subversive attempts comparable to those of the last years of the Peloponnesian war. It would be a distortion of reality to present Eubulos and his friends as anything other than 'pacifists'; the term 'moderates' scarcely fits them, in so far as there is no trace, during the period when they dominated Athenian political life, between 356 and 346, of any effort to limit the omnipotence of the Assembly and the courts. Aeschines, the chief orator of the 'Macedonian' party, even when he happens to complain vigorously of the degradation of political life in his time—which Demosthenes also does—never calls in question the essential principle of popular sovereignty, and in this, too, he is at one with Demosthenes. The only arguments on which one might base an identification of the Macedonian party with the oligarchic party are, on the one hand, the decree of Eukrates immediately following Chaironea, and on the other the personal role of Phokion from 338 onward and the decree of Antipater in 322. We shall return to this question later. In any case, however, these facts are all subsequent to the defeat, and it would be wholly arbitrary to cite them in reference to the period before 340. One is thus forced to the conclusion that the anti-

Macedonian orators' arguments are invalid. Unlike the Spartans, Philip, unfamiliar with the world of the Athenian *polis*, had no reason to uphold one form of political regime rather than another, and if in Athens some who still hankered after an oligarchy hoped that defeat might favour their endeavours, they were not likely to have sought to influence Philip in that direction.

However, one can see the interest that Philip's adversaries may have had in using this argument. To invoke the dangers threatening democracy was, like the appeal to the memory of their illustrious ancestors and their city's glorious past, an argument calculated to arouse the emotions of the crowd and to affect the decisions of the Assembly. Moreover, in order to oblige the rich to finance the war effort and the poor to agree to give up the *theorikon*, it was useful to be able to present the struggle against Philip as a political one.

In this conflict, the anti-Macedonian orators were assured of the support of certain *strategoi* such as Chares, eager to resume their part in a battle in which they hoped to win glory, prestige and wealth. There were undoubtedly close connections between Chares and Demosthenes, and the unconditional support given by Demosthenes to Diopeithes was to find expression in the speech *On the Chersonese*. The question obviously arises how far Demosthenes acted as spokesman for Chares and his group. It is not impossible that at the start of his political career he may have acted, at first, on behalf of the 'imperialist' faction; but gradually, as his personality developed and as his role in the *polis* became more important, he unquestionably came to defend Athens' freedom of action rather than the now hopeless notion of hegemony. A comparison between his first speeches and those which preceded the final battle is significant in this respect: the evocation of a glorious past, memories of his readings of Thucydides are replaced by a far more realistic view of immediate necessities, and increasingly concrete and precise proposals. In this respect, just as the 'Macedonian' party is to be distinguished from the supporters of pacifism or oligarchy, so the 'anti-Macedonian' party cannot be identified with any democratic or imperialist group, and it is not surprising that a moderate such as Lykourgos should have stood by the side of Demosthenes in the struggle against Philip. Personal friendships, immediate interests, a greater or less degree of perspicacity as to what was needed to maintain the balance of the *polis*, may have determined a variety of options and attitudes.

An assumption which is plainly unfounded as regards prominent individuals, however, acquires some justification when we consider the underlying levels of society, as the struggle against Philip came to require the mobilization of ever greater amounts of energy and resources. Men of wealth and property, the principal victims of the war effort, eventually envisaged peace with Macedonia as the guarantee of their security, backed by a system of restricted franchise, the necessity for which was urged upon them by a whole group of intellectuals.

The principles of democracy called in question by political thinkers [11]

The fourth century represents a crucial period in the history of Greek political thought. True, the second half of the fifth century had already witnessed a confrontation between supporters and opponents of the political regime in which the supreme power lay in the hands of the multitude, the *plethos*. The *Athenaion Politeia*, an anonymous (pseudo-Xenophon) pamphlet published shortly before the outbreak of the Peloponnesian war, had sketched in its broad lines what was to be the credo of the opponents of democracy. It asserted:

> Everywhere on earth the best element is opposed to democracy. For among the best people there is minimal wantonness and injustice but a maximum of scrupulous care for what is good, whereas among the people there is a maximum of ignorance, disorder and wickedness; for poverty draws them rather to disgraceful actions, and because of a lack of money some men are uneducated and ignorant (I, 5). . . . In the courts [the people] are not so much concerned with justice as with their own advantage . . . they disfranchise the aristocrats, take away their money, expel and kill them, whereas they promote the interests of the lower class (I, 13, 14). . . . Further, for oligarchic cities it is necessary to keep to alliances and oaths. If they do not abide by agreements or if injustice is done, there are the names of the few who made the agreement. But whatever agreements the populace makes can be repudiated by referring the blame to the one who spoke or took the vote, while the others declare that they were absent or did not approve of the agreement made in the full assembly. If it seems advisable for their decisions not to be

effective, they invent myriad excuses for not doing what they do not want to do. And if there are any bad results from the people's plans, they charge that a few persons, working against them, ruined their plans; but if there is a good result, they take the credit for themselves (II, 17).

The ignorance of the *demos*, the unfairness of its judgments where the rich and respectable are concerned, the fickleness of Assemblies and their lack of any sense of responsibility, such are the arguments which we find repeated by the opponents of democracy throughout the fourth century.

Among these, however, certain distinctions must be made. On the one hand there were the 'philosophers', those disciples of Plato at the Academy and of Aristotle at the Lyceum who compared the respective merits of various constitutions and were thereby led to analyse and judge the democratic regime, as they knew it in the everyday reality of Athenian life. On the other, there were men like Isokrates or Xenophon, closer to those who played an active part in politics and therefore more inclined to argue from concrete facts, to neglect principles and confine themselves to actualities. The opinions of the first group were more absolute, in one sense, but less definitive, whereas the indictment of the second group was more categorical because their point of departure was less theoretical.

It is obviously impossible within the limits of the present work to make an exhaustive analysis of Greek political thought in the fourth century. We shall merely examine the various complaints already made in the pseudo-Xenophon pamphlet and see how each is developed by the writers of the fourth century.

It is clear that the first complaint, that the *demos* sets itself up as judge of things of which it is ignorant, constitutes for Plato the essential argument against democracy. Since 'it is impossible for the people to be philosophical', that is to say capable of judging beauty and ugliness, justice and injustice, or of attaining real knowledge, therefore democracy, which subjects every issue to the judgment of the people, is a regime whose very principle is at fault. Here Plato echoes themes which were already widespread (cf. Herodotos III, 81; Euripides, *Suppliant Women*, 412 ff.), but which he supports by his general theory of knowledge. Other political writers of the fourth century were less categorical in their indictment. Aristotle even went so far as to admit that the crowd, although its components might be of mediocre quality, might have a certain superiority over the individual, however gifted: 'For it is possible that the many, though not individually good men, yet when they come together may be better, not individually but collectively' (*Politics*, 1281a 40–1281b).

As for Isokrates, he wrote of democracy:

> I know that under this constitution our ancestors were far superior to the rest of the world . . . Moreover, if we will examine the history of the most illustrious and the greatest of the other states we shall find that democratic forms of government are more advantageous for them than oligarchies. For if we compare our own government . . . not with the democracy which I have described [i.e. that of the ancestors] but with the rule which was instituted by the Thirty, there is no one who would not consider our present democracy a divine creation (*Areopagiticus*, 61–2).

Moreover, the political writers of the fourth century condemned the way democracy was practised, and above all the fickleness of Assemblies on the one hand, the unfairness of popular judgments, particularly towards the rich, on the other. Already at the beginning of the century Aristophanes had compared the Assembly's decrees to the actions of drunken men. Forty years later Isokrates wrote in *On the Peace*:

> We are so devoid of reason that we do not hold the same views about the same question on the same day. On the contrary, the things which we condemn before we enter the assembly are the very things which we vote for when we are in session, and again a little later when we depart to our homes we disapprove of the things which we resolved upon here (52).

The inconsistency of popular decisions was further aggravated by a lack of respect for the laws. Plato writes in the *Republic* that the citizens of a 'democratic city' enjoy '. . . freedom from all compulsion to hold office in such a city, even if you are qualified, or again, to submit to rule, unless you please, or to make war when the rest are at war, or to keep the peace when the others do so, unless you desire peace' (557e). Aristotle echoes him in the *Politics*: 'One mark of liberty which all democrats set down as a principle of the constitution . . . is for a man to live as he likes, for they say that this is the function of liberty (1317b, 11–13). Isokrates, in the *Panathenaicus*, defines contemporary democracy as 'the kind which operates at haphazard, mistaking licence for liberty and freedom to do what one likes for happiness' (131). The thirst for liberty taken to its extreme limits leads the citizens to 'pay no heed even to the laws written or unwritten, so that . . . they may have no master anywhere over them' (Plato, *Republic*, 563d). Xenophon moreover, in the *Memorabilia*, justifies, through the mouth of Perikles, the omnipotence of the *demos*: 'Laws are all the rules approved and enacted by the majority in the assembly, whereby they declare what ought and what ought not to be done' (I, 2, 42).

How, then, can one be surprised at the inconsistency of popular decisions, and of the boundless power available to those who, by flattering the *demos*, lead it in paths that are often contradictory and always harmful? 'We pretend that we are the wisest of the Hellenes, but we employ the kind of advisers whom no one could fail to despise, and we place those very same men in control of all our public interests to whom no one would entrust a single one of his private affairs' (Isokrates, *On the Peace*, 52).

This inconsistency, this contempt for law, this susceptibility to the influence of demagogues are not wholly gratuitous: they are aimed at despoiling the rich for the benefit of the multitude and above all of its bad counsellors. This is in fact the accusation which we find repeated by all fourth-century writers, identifying democracy with government by the poor. Plato writes in Book VIII of the *Republic*: '. . . a democracy comes into being when the poor, winning the victory, put to death some of the other party, drive out others, and grant the rest of the citizens an equal share in both citizenship and offices' (557a). Aristotle's definition runs: 'It is a democracy when those who are free are in the majority and have sovereignty over the government, and an oligarchy when the rich and more well-born are few and sovereign' (*Politics*, 1290b, 17–18).

As for Isokrates, he sees the results of this situation: the rich are overburdened, demagogues lead the people as they choose by dazzling them with the promise of more or less imaginary material advantages.

I marvel that you cannot see at once that no class is so inimical to the people as our depraved orators and demagogues. For, as if your other misfortunes were not enough, their chief desire is that you should be in want of your daily necessities, observing that those who are able to manage their affairs from their private incomes are on the side of the commonwealth and of our best counsellors, whereas those who live off the lawcourts and the assemblies and the doles derived from them are constrained by their need to be subservient to the sycophants, and are deeply grateful for the impeachments and the indictments and the other sharp practices which are due to the sycophants. Wherefore these men would be most happy to see all our citizens reduced to the condition of helplessness in which they themselves are powerful (*On the Peace*, 129–131).

These complaints by the well-to-do are echoed all through the century, and form not the least of the objections raised by political thinkers against democracy. Already in the *Oeconomicus* of Xenophon we find Socrates pitying his wealthy interlocutor, Kritoboulos, for being subjected to great expenses in order to avoid the hostility of his compatriots, and Isokrates enumerated the many burdens which the city-state inflicted on the rich, who were moreover ready-made victims for tribunals and informers.

We have already seen what substance underlay these accusations. It may be of interest to recall the means by which theoreticians proposed to counter these evils. Plato, as we have said, condemned the very principle of democracy: for him, there could not be any sort of improvement of the regime; only education and a new organization of the *polis* could provide the remedy for the ills from which Greece suffered. We can undoubtedly recognize an evolution from the utopia of the *Republic* to the highly precise and minute account of the institutions of the city of the Magnetes, and the close relationship between the *polis* depicted in the *Laws* and the institutions of Athens has frequently been pointed out.[12] The fact remains, however, that the colony of the Magnetes, precisely because it was a colony, could be developed on the basis of a special social and economic structure, differing fundamentally from that which Athens had acquired through the course of her long history, and that in particular the problem of the antagonism between rich and poor did not arise, since a certain equality and mediocrity of fortune was laid down from the start. Thus there were only two essential necessities to be stressed: education, on which everything depended, and the safeguarding of the laws. The other political writers of the fourth century, being less categorical in their indictment, were more concerned to find remedies that might make democracy acceptable. For Xenophon, when he wrote *Ways and Means* on his return to Athens, peace and a judicious exploitation of all the resources of the city-state would enable democracy to recover its right balance: the rich would be released from the burden of trierarchies and property-taxes, the poor would benefit from the increased wealth of the city; we have seen that the project of the mass purchase of miner-slaves was born from the idea of providing every citizen with his three obols a day—an unrealizable project, indeed, but one which for the first time made the welfare of all dependent on an 'economic' project.

For Isokrates, too, peace was an essential factor, and we have already referred to the close connection between *Ways and Means* and *On the Peace*, but in his view the restoration of peace, although it might bring back prosperity, was not in itself enough to make democracy acceptable, unless accompanied by a reform of political morality. This could only be achieved if, as of old, the Areopagus were to stand surety for it. It is hardly necessary to underline the historical inaccuracies accumulated by Isokrates in his attempt to strengthen his propaganda in favour of Athens' leading tribunal with arguments drawn from an imagined past; but it must be admitted that much uncertainty still exists as to the real role which that ancient aristocratic court was repeatedly called upon to play during the course of the century. Isokrates launches into a stirring eulogy of the Areopagus and of its role as guardian of order and morality, but the main point of the reforms he suggested consisted, in fact, in the choice of the city's rulers: these were no longer to be drawn by lot, but appointed on grounds of ability:

What contributed most to their [i.e. the ancestors'] good government of the state was that of the two recognized kinds of equality—that which makes the same award to all alike and that which gives to each man his due—they did not fail to grasp which was the more service-able; but rejecting as unjust that which holds that the good and the bad are worthy of the same honours, and preferring rather that which rewards and punishes every man according to his deserts, they governed the city on this principle, not filling the offices by lot from all the citizens, but selecting the best and the ablest for each function of the state; for they believed that the rest of the people would reflect the character of those who were placed in charge of their affairs . . . Furthermore, they considered that this way of appointing magistrates was also more democratic than the casting of

65

lots, since under the plan of election by lot chance would decide the issue and the partisans of oligarchy would often get the offices; whereas under the plan of selecting the worthiest men, the people would have in their hands the power to choose those who were most attached to the existing constitution (*Areopagiticus*, 23).

The 'worthiest' (*tous epieikestatous*) were obviously the rich. Isokrates did not say so in so many words, for this would have exposed him to the indictment of extolling oligarchy. He confined himself to wishing that people of inferior station should devote themselves to agriculture and trade, whereas horsemanship, gymnastics, hunting and . . . philosophy were the exclusive province of the rich (ibid. 44). Aristotle, however, who, writing a few years later, could express himself more freely, did not hesitate to recommend a reform of the magistrature which meant, in fact, that posts would be reserved for those who did not seek to use them to increase their own power and wealth—in other words for those who already possessed both of these. To reserve access to the magistrature to wealthy men, while allowing the *demos* as a whole the right to elect magistrates, meant respecting popular sovereignty and at the same time preventing the exercise of authority from becoming a means to self-enrichment. What was sought, as we see, was not a total rejection of democracy, but a return to ancient practices which the radical nature of Athenian democracy had caused to disappear.

We may obviously question the soundness of these criticisms and of the solutions recommended. As we have already seen, although certain *strategoi* may have taken advantage of their authority to enrich themselves unfairly, most of them were, on the contrary, obliged to pledge their property in order to meet their obligations. There is no reason to suppose that the franchise restrictions existing in the preceding century had been completely abandoned; and the adversaries of democracy could easily take advantage of a few exceptional cases to advocate a return to a much stricter system of restricted franchise, which would eventually deprive the majority not only of the few offices open to them but of the exercise of citizenship itself.

However, no one dared to suggest this openly in the Athens of Demosthenes, on pain of being accused of intriguing against the regime, and the criticisms of theoreticians were made only within a narrow circle of privileged listeners, who, when they passed from theory to practice, promptly identified themselves with the 'system': witness Kallistratos and Timotheos. Others turned aside from active politics. Others, again, finally, tried experiments elsewhere, in which they strove to introduce a little of their masters' teaching, as for instance Harmias of Atarneus, Aristotle's friend; but the chief factor of that teaching which they retained was the indictment of ignorant rulers. Short of a complete reorganization of the *polis* on a model more or less directly inspired from Sparta, it was impossible to envisage a wholesale education of the *demos*. Hence the education system, the *paideia*, must remain a privilege reserved for a small number, an elite not of birth or fortune but of learning. But in the last resort, such an elite could be imposed only if a man of superior quality assumed responsibility for the fate of the *polis*. It is not surprising, under these circumstances, to find a theoretical condemnation of democracy leading to a vindication of monarchical power: timidly expressed, since it was not possible to advocate the authority of one individual in a city-state where this was identified with that detested regime, tyranny, but expressed none the less, by Plato (*Politics*), Xenophon (*Kyropaedia*, *Hieron*, *Agesilaus*), Isokrates (*Nikokles*, *Philip*) and Aristotle, although by some paradox of history Aristotle, who was tutor to Alexander, was the most reluctant to envisage monarchy as a possible regime within the framework of the *polis*.[13]

In point of fact, it was outside that framework that a 'royal' monarchy was to develop, with Alexander to begin with and then with his successors, who, heirs to the sovereigns of the ancient East, were to combine that heritage with the teaching of Athenian philosophers.[14] The independent Greek city-state which had been characteristic of the civilization of the Aegean since the eighth century, and of which Athens appeared to theoreticians as the symbolic embodiment, was no longer capable of solving its internal problems, and its defeat by the Macedonian was to mark the end of a critical period in the history of human civilization, that which saw the flowering of a particular form of political community, to which the Athenian political writers of the fourth century, by their very opposition to the democratic regime, bear witness.

Chaironea and the end of Greek liberty

As we have already seen, Philip's ventures in the northern Aegean and in central Greece had at first been assisted by the dissension existing between Greek cities. But early in 340 B.C. the relentless propaganda of Demosthenes had borne fruit: a coalition had been formed, centring round Athens, to meet the challenge of the Macedonian king. The precarious peace which had existed since 346 B.C. was about to be shattered.

The war In the summer of 340 Philip set off towards the Hellespont with a fleet and an army. Having left some troops in the Chersonese, he besieged Perinth, which received prompt assistance from the Great King and from Byzantium. Despite the use of powerful siege engines Philip did not succeed in taking the town, and to prevent it from receiving further help he turned to invest Byzantium. At the same time he sent a letter to the Athenians, which Demosthenes considered as nothing less than an ultimatum. It listed all his grievances against Athens, complaining in particular of Diopeithes' plundering forays and of the negotiations being carried on by Athens with Persia.

This meant open war. Philip's first act of aggression was to seize merchant ships crossing through the Straits under the protection of the Athenian fleet. Chares was promptly sent at the head of a fleet of forty ships to bring aid to the Byzantines; but they refused to receive the *strategos*, remembering his hostile operations at the time of the war against the allies. A new fleet had therefore to be sent, under the command of Kephisophon and Phokion, to whom the Byzantines consented to entrust the defence of their city. It is interesting in this connection to recall a story mentioned by Plutarch: Phokion's entry into the city was facilitated by the friendly relations he had maintained with his fellow-student at the Academy, Leon, who was an influential Byzantine orator.[15] Meanwhile, the allies of Athens also sent aid to Byzantium: Chios, Rhodes, Kos and the Great King, the last providing principally subsidies. Philip was obliged to raise his siege of Perinth and of Byzantium, but he was able to bring his fleet back into the Aegean without hindrance. Shortly afterwards he concluded peace with Perinth and Byzantium and took advantage of the respite offered by winter to prepare an assault on the Skythians of the Lower Danube. It was on his return from this expedition that he was wounded during an engagement with the Triballi.

During that same winter, war preparations had been going on in Athens. Already the previous year, before the interruption of the peace of Philokrates, Demosthenes had put through a law ending the organization of trierarchical groupings instituted by Periander in 357. As we have seen, the effect of this law had been to make the burden of the trierarchy fall on a larger number of well-to-do Athenians and consequently to relieve the richest group. Demosthenes re-established the ancient system, not without encountering violent opposition. A suit was even brought against him by one Patrokles of Phtya, but Demosthenes was acquitted:

> Now how much money do you think the first, second and third classes of contributors on the Naval Boards offered me not to propose the measures, or failing that, to put it on the list and then drop it on demurrer? It was so large a sum, men of Athens, that I hardly like to name it. It was natural that they should make this attempt. Under the former statutes they might discharge their public services in groups of sixteen, spending little or nothing themselves, but grinding down the needy citizens, whereas by my statute they had to return the full assessment according to their means, and a man who was formerly one of sixteen contributors to a single trireme . . . might have to furnish two complete vessels (Demosthenes, *On the Crown*, 103–4).

It was no doubt during the year 339 that Demosthenes succeeded at last in having the theoric funds transferred to the military exchequer. He himself became 'Commissioner of the Fleet', while another anti-Macedonian orator, Lykourgos, was made responsible for administering the military fund.

The orator's chief aim was to provide Athens with a fleet capable of keeping Philip away for ever from the region which was vital for Athens' supplies. The king of Macedonia, however, was astute enough to make land rather than sea the decisive theatre of operations, by reopening the 'sacred war'. At the meeting of the Amphiktyonic Council in the spring, the West Lokrians had set down a complaint against the Athenians on a fallacious pretext: the inscription on the golden shields offered to the goddess was, they claimed, insulting to the Thebans, allies of the Persians. Aeschines was one of the three *pylagorai* representing Athens at the meeting, the other two being Midias and Thrasykles of Oion. Anxious, so he professed, to avoid a rupture with the Thebans and also to reject the humiliation inflicted on his city, he diverted the wrath of the Amphiktyonic League against these same Lokrians, accusing the men of Amphissa of sacrilege for having tilled the sacred plain of Kirrha and levied taxes on ships entering the port. A punitive expedition was promptly sent against the Amphissians, as prelude to a fresh 'sacred war'. This was decided on by an extraordinary assembly, held in June in Thermopylai, to which the Athenians, as the result of a motion proposed by Demosthenes and approved by the *demos*, had sent no representatives.

A few years later, during the lawsuit on the Crown, Aeschines and Demosthenes were to give diametrically opposed interpretations of this affair. According to Aeschines, the main object was to avert the anger of the Amphiktyonic League from Athens and to punish an authentic sacrilege. In refusing to send delegates to the Assembly of Thermopylai, the Athenians, misled by Demosthenes, whom everyone knew to be in the pay of the Amphissians, had made a grave mistake. According to Demosthenes, on the contrary, Aeschines was well aware when he accused the Amphissians that he was helping Philip to strengthen his position in central Greece.

> The war of Amphissa, that is, the war that brought Philip to Elatea, and caused the election, as general of the Amphiktyons, of a man who turned all Greece upside down, was due to the machinations of this man. In his own single person he was the author of all our worst evils (*On the Crown*, 143).

In fact, the Sacred War was to provide Philip with the pretext for aggressive action against those Greek cities which had, like Athens, refused to associate themselves with it, or which, like Thebes, had a traditional alliance with the West Lokrians. Even before the regular meeting of the Amphiktyonic Council at the beginning of September, at which Philip was to be entrusted with the direction of operations, the Thebans had driven the Macedonian garrison out of Nikaia in West Lokris. This hostile act, and the need to protect his rear, impelled Philip to act promptly. He had been appointed supreme commander, he was convinced of his rights, and he seized Elatea in order to cut the road between Thebes and Nikaia. The operation was performed swiftly, and it caused temporary stupefaction in Athens. The Assembly was hastily summoned, and Demosthenes, seeing all the advantage he could get from the event, persuaded the Athenians to send an embassy to Thebes with himself at its head. When the Athenian ambassadors arrived in Boiotia they found that they had been forestalled by an embassy from Philip's allies within the Amphiktyonic Council. In order to secure the alliance, they had to agree to entrust the leadership of the land forces to the Boiotians, while Athens undertook to pay two-thirds of the cost of the war and to recognize the authority of the Boiotian League over all the cities of Boiotia, in particular over Oropos.

Aeschines did not fail to blame his adversary for these concessions.

> What brought you into Thebes was the crisis and fear and the need of alliance, not Demosthenes. For in this whole affair Demosthenes is responsible to you for three most serious mistakes. The first was this: Philip was nominally making war against you, but really was far more the enemy of Thebes, as the event itself has proved. Demosthenes concealed these facts, which were so important, and pretending that the alliance was to be brought about, not through the crisis but through his own negotiations, first he persuaded the people to give up all consideration of the terms of the alliance, and to count themselves fortunate if only it were made; and when he had gained this point he betrayed all Boiotia to the Thebans, by writing in the decree: 'If any city refuse to follow Thebes, the Athenians shall aid the Boiotians in Thebes' . . . Secondly he laid two-thirds of the costs of the war upon you, whose danger was more remote, and only one third on the Thebans (in all this acting for bribes); and the leadership by sea he caused to be shared equally by both, but all the expenditure he laid upon you; and the leadership by land . . . he handed over to Thebes. The result was that in all the war that followed, Stratokles, your general, had no authority to plan for the safety of his troops . . . (*Against Ktesiphon*, 141–3).

Aeschines enumerated the other manoeuvres through which, in his view, Demosthenes led the Greeks to their downfall: sending mercenaries to the Amphissians, refusing Philip's final peace offers, and so on. Needless to say, speaking nine years after the event, Aeschines had every opportunity of denouncing the 'mistakes' of Demosthenes. The latter, in his reply, none the less justified a policy which, even if it had been unable to avert the final defeat, had at least borne fruit in the immediate present:

> We owe it to that policy of mine which he denounces that, instead of the Thebans joining Philip in an invasion of our country, as every-

one expected, they fought by our side and stopped him; that, instead of the seat of war being in Attica, it was seven hundred furlongs away on the far side of Boiotia; that, instead of privateers from Euboea harrying us, Attica was at peace on the sea-frontier throughout the war; and that, instead of Philip taking Byzantium and holding the Hellespont, the Byzantines fought on our side against him . . . (*On the Crown*, 229–30).

In point of fact, the winter which followed the conclusion of the alliance between Athens and Thebes passed without any important operation affecting the balance of forces. In the diplomatic field, alliances were concluded with the Achaean League, Corinth, Megara, the Euboean cities, etc. Negotiations proposed by Philip were rejected, on the prompting of Demosthenes. Athens could feel safe both on land and at sea.

However, in the middle of the summer of 338 Philip decided to take the offensive. He seized Amphissa, ravaged Boiotian territory and took Naupaktos. Controlling the main strategic points, he then gave battle against the allied armies in the plain of Chaironea (late August–early September 338). The sequel is well known: having broken the right wing, where the Boiotians were massed, Philip was able to attack the Athenians, who formed the left wing, in the rear. The result was total defeat, followed almost immediately by the occupation of Thebes and the establishment of a Macedonian garrison in the Kadmeia.[16]

Athens after Chaironea—the decree of Hypereides and the Peace of Demades　The short period between the defeat at Chaironea and the conclusion of the so-called Peace of Demades constitutes an important, if little known, episode in the history of Athens in the fourth century. Most written evidence is posterior to the event; the only contemporary texts are the speech of Lykourgos against Leokrates, fragments of Hypereides and an allusion by Demosthenes in the second speech against Aristogeiton.

Unquestionably, when the news of the defeat reached Athens, panic ensued. Indeed, it seemed certain that Philip was preparing for Athens a punishment similar to that which he had recently inflicted on Thebes. The orators of the anti-Macedonian party, among their leaders being Hypereides, who was then a member of the *Boule*, and Demosthenes himself, made the hastily summoned Assembly adopt a series of measures for 'public safety': the rural population were to be provided with shelter within the city walls, the *Boule* was to remain in permanent session, in arms, in the Piraeus, elder citizens were to be mobilized to keep guard on the ramparts, exiles to be recalled and *atimoi*, disfranchised people, to have their civic rights restored.[17] These measures were comparable to those taken immediately after Aigospotamoi and on every occasion when the city had been seriously threatened. There was nothing essentially illegal about them, such as could have justified an indictment by the opponents of Hypereides, if indeed that orator was responsible for them; but these traditional defence measures were accompanied by provisions which might well provoke an accusation of illegality. Hypereides was said to have proposed, in order to increase the number of those taking part in the common defence of the city, to grant citizenship to metics and freedom to the slaves who volunteered.[18] We have only fragments of the speech he delivered in his own defence during the action brought against him by the informer Aristogeiton:

> What is the use of these reiterated questions about the part I played? 'Did you propose to give freedom to slaves?'—Yes, so that free men should not have to endure slavery.—'Did you propose to restore the right of citizenship to those who had lost it?'—Yes, so that all Athenians with a single heart should fight for their country.—'Did you propose the recall of exiles?'—Yes, so that no one should have to suffer exile.—'Did you not read the laws which conflicted with your proposals?'—I could not read them, for the Macedonians' weapons, rising up in front of them, hid them from me with their shadow (fragment 27–8, Jensen).

The freeing of the slaves and the granting of citizenship to the metics who took part in the defence of the *polis* were obviously emergency measures. There is no reason to assume that the democratic leaders were acting on principle; but neither, perhaps, should we minimize the importance of such measures, which prove that for some Athenians the difference between a citizen and a resident alien was not an insurmountable one.[19] As for the arming of slaves, while other examples of this can be cited—in Sicily for instance, at the time of Dionysios—it reveals the gulf then dividing political men at grips with reality from theoreticians arguing about abstract ideas. The social fact of slavery was not being challenged, but the actual situation in fourth-century Athens made it possible to associate its slaves with the patriotic struggle.

As for the fighting force which such a proposal would have provided, had it been implemented, it would have amounted to some 150,000 men. This number, often cited by scholars seeking to assess the size of the slave population of Athens, cannot be accepted unquestioningly. One can scarcely imagine Athens capable of equipping so large an army overnight, and there could be no question of depriving agriculture and industry of the major part of their manpower, even for a limited period.

We know that Hypereides' proposal was attacked by Aristogeiton, who brought a suit against him.[20] The trial took place, for we possess fragments of Hypereides' defence. But the chronology of events is too uncertain for a precise date to be offered.

Furthermore, we do not know whether it was at this time that the Areopagus was granted emergency powers, and to what end. Our only evidence here comes from Plutarch's *Life of Phokion*, where he writes:

> When the defeat came and the turbulent and revolutionary spirits in the city dragged Charidemos to the tribunal and demanded that he be made general, the best citizens were filled with fear; and with the aid of the council of the Areopagos in the assembly, by dint of entreaties and tears, they persuaded them at last to entrust the city to the guidance of Phokion (16).

Indubitably, a certain unrest must have prevailed in Athens at this time, and the antagonism between the supporters and the adversaries of Philip must have sharpened. As we have already seen, it would be wrong to identify the pro-Macedonian party, before Chaironea, with that of the opponents of democracy. It is not impossible, however, that the unrest which followed the defeat may have contributed to a stiffening of attitudes. All those who felt uneasy about the popular agitation that centred round the figure of Charidemos may well have hoped that an immediate peace with Philip, negotiated through the intermediary of men of the pro-Macedonian party, would bring about the swift restoration of internal order.

This explains the favourable reception given to the proposals brought by Demades and the rapid conclusion of the Peace. Philip, not unaware of Athens' potential strength, might hope to have her for an ally, especially if a number of Athenians were prepared to stand guarantee for her docility—whence the remarkably favourable terms of the Peace of Demades. Philip undertook to send no troops into Attica and no ships into the Piraeus. He left Athens in possession of the islands where she had cleruchies, of Delos and of Samos. He further made her a present of Oropos, much to the satisfaction of those who had not looked with favour on the alliance with the Boiotian League, for which so high a price had been paid. Prisoners of war were to be sent home without ransom, and the ashes of the dead solemnly brought back to Athens. The only unfavourable condition was the abandonment of the alliance, but since 357 this had been almost moribund, and the sacrifice was therefore not a great one.

The League of Corinth and the death of Philip The peace proposals were ratified, apparently without serious opposition from the orators of the anti-Macedonian party. A few months later, in the spring of 337, the Congress of Corinth was held. Philip had invited the Greek city-states to send delegates with the aim of concluding a treaty and a general peace. In Athens, Philip's proposal, upheld before the Assembly by Demades, had aroused opposition from some members, including, unexpectedly, Phokion.[21] The *strategos* was in fact apprehensive as to the financial burden which a joint war against the barbarian would render necessary, and we may assume that he had behind him a number of wealthy Athenians who had with some reluctance borne the weight of the war against Philip, and were presumably not anxious to incur the expense of a new war waged, this time, at Philip's side. However, for the great majority of the Athenians, the prospect of an easy war, which promised rich booty, under the leadership of so illustrious a general, was a tempting one. As for those who had been affected by the propaganda of Isokrates, they could not but rejoice at seeing the old orator's dream come true at last. For after hoping for so long that Athens would be in a position to achieve the unity of the Greek world, with herself as centre, and bring to a successful conclusion the struggle against the barbarian and the conquest of Asia, which alone would make it possible to end the ills from which Greece was suffering, Isokrates had come at last to support Philip, seeing in him the only man capable of settling the futile disputes between the city-states and of leading them, united, towards the conquest of Asia.

The Congress of Corinth ratified a general peace and led to the conclusion of a treaty of alliance of which Philip did not actually form part, but whose supreme leader he became.[22] The aim of this alliance was to renew the struggle against the barbarian in order to obtain vengeance for the misdeeds committed by the Persians during Xerxes' wars. This is not the place to study the way it functioned, which in any case remains little known; but we cannot fail to be surprised at Philip's adoption of a theme of Athenian propaganda which in any case had long been abandoned. We can see that this provided him with a sure means of winning over the public opinion of the Greeks, in particular of the Athenians, when we consider the suspicion still aroused among them by any hint of a *rapprochement* with Persia. We know the use that Demosthenes' adversaries were to make against him of his supposed association with the Great King.

We can therefore scarcely wonder if during the months that followed the conclusion of the treaty of alliance, the *demos* ratified a certain number of decrees or proposals in Philip's favour. He was granted the right of Athenian citizenship, while certain of his devoted supporters, Euthykrates of Olynthos, the *strategos* Alkimachos, and possibly Antipater, were made *proxenoi*. A decree, quoted by Diodoros, laid down that anyone making an attempt on the life of Philip would be denied refuge in Athens (XVI, 92, 1–2). Finally, a statue of Philip was to be set up on the Agora.

It is in this context that we must try to explain the terms of a decree, recently discovered, which has been interpreted as a hostile measure against the Macedonian and his supporters. This is the decree of Eukrates, which laid down severe penalties against anyone attempting to overthrow the democracy and restore tyranny, and particularly against members of the Areopagus encouraging such a manoeuvre.[23] This decree is dated from the archonship of Phrynichos. It is thus contemporary with the proxeny-decrees in favour of eminent Macedonians. Its author, Eukrates, was to die in 322, a victim of the hostility of Antipater. To conclude from this that the decree emanated from sections of the people who were hostile to the alliance with Macedonia is but a short step, which most commentators on the decree have readily taken, concluding with the following analysis: After the defeat at Chaironea the Macedonian party sought to gain control of the *polis* by setting at its head a tyrant docile to Philip's orders. The people's party, led by Eukrates, had countered these manoeuvres by promoting a decree directed particularly against those Areopagites whose complicity with the Macedonian party was blatant.

Such an interpretation is worth considering. As we have already said, great caution must be observed in identifying the opponents of the regime with the supporters of Philip. Even if measures such as those propounded by Hypereides may have aroused the anxiety of moderates and the well-to-do, throwing them into the arms of Philip, there is no proof that they wished to forearm themselves against the return of such a danger by altering the regime. Peace had been concluded advantageously for Athens; Philip's demands were not inordinate and the honours granted him had been approved by the *demos*. It is hard to see what interest Philip and his partisans would have had in establishing a tyranny in Athens, particularly since among prominent Athenians the man who seemed most faithful to the Macedonian alliance, Phokion, did not appear apt to fill the role of tyrant.

It is important, moreover, not to lose sight of the fact that in the fourth century tyranny was invariably associated with popular revolution: the tyrant was the man who abolished debts, shared out lands, freed slaves and had the support of the bulk of the poor. Obviously, when describing such a tyrant, Athenian political writers had in mind certain contemporary examples rather than the regime which had once held sway over Athens, and against a return of which democracy, once it had triumphed, had forearmed itself by ostracism in the first place, then by certain legislative provisions. Athens had apparently known no such threat during the fourth century; but on several occasions popular unrest had made the democratic rulers apprehensive. The measures proposed by Hypereides were, to be sure, emergency measures, but in the context of the fourth century they had a 'tyrannical' aspect which could not fail to arouse anxiety. We must also recall what Plutarch said of the situation in Athens after its defeat: 'When the turbulent and revolutionary spirits in the city dragged Charidemos to the tribunal and demanded that he be made general, the best citizens were filled with fear.' We may ask, consequently, whether the decree of Eukrates, far from being a measure directed against Philip and his supporters, was not on the contrary aimed against those elements in the *polis* which might have been favourable to a revolution leading to tyranny. I have even suggested [24] that possibly, in this respect, it may have formed part of the provisions advocated by Philip when the Corinthian

League was formed, and which we know from a speech attributed to Demosthenes: Philip had in fact asked the Greeks to pledge their word not to undertake 'any postponement, any division of land, any liberation of slaves for a revolutionary end'. I am no longer so sure that a connection ought to be made between the two facts, for it seems that, at least until 322, political conflicts do not necessarily coincide with the problem of relations with the Macedonian king. The recollection of recent events, of Hypereides' proposal, of the manoeuvres in favour of Charidemos, are perhaps sufficient to explain the renewed enforcement of provisions which might have fallen into neglect.

One problem remains, however—that of the mention of the Areopagites in the decree. The traditional interpretation is plausible enough: the Areopagus, which was essentially a conservative organ, may have been involved in intrigues conducted by Philip's supporters. Plutarch's text, quoted above, provides a supplementary argument in favour of this thesis: it was with the support of the Areopagus that the wealthy succeeded in thrusting aside Charidemos and securing the government of the *polis* for Phokion (with the title of *strategos autokrator*?). But once again, nothing justifies one in supposing that Phokion aspired to the tyranny, and moreover, even though he had been a member of the embassy that made peace with Philip, there is no indication that he exercised any special power in Athens at that time. Even if for a few months he was granted full powers to avoid the spread of popular unrest, this authority does not appear to have been maintained. The situation had become normal once more at the time when the Assembly adopted Eukrates' decree, and the part played then by such men as Demosthenes, Hypereides or Lykourgos proves that Phokion did not exercise any sort of tyranny on Philip's behalf. As for the alliance of the Areopagites with the Macedonian party, this does not stand up to examination. We know that the Areopagus had chosen Hypereides in preference to Aeschines to represent the city-state at Delphi, and it was by the Areopagus that Demosthenes wished to be judged on the occasion of the Harpalos affair. None the less, one would like to know exactly what were the powers of Athens' leading tribunal at that time. Unquestionably, they had been strengthened, just as after Aigospotamoi at the end of the fifth century. This can be interpreted in a very definite sense: in tragic circumstances, the Areopagus became once more the guardian of the constitution. We can thus understand both its intervention against the 'tyrannical' manoeuvres of Charidemos, and the fact that it is mentioned in the decree of Eukrates. It was because the Areopagites were guardians of the constitution that any threat to it might reflect upon them. Eukrates' decree does not therefore necessarily imply the existence of any danger of tyranny based on the Macedonian party in Athens in the months that followed the conclusion of the Corinthian League, nor express the reaction of a popular patriotic party against such a threat. It reveals merely a certain unrest, the causes of which cannot be imputed solely to defeat, and which marks the beginning of an imbalance which was to worsen during the years that followed.

Philip was to die soon afterwards, assassinated on the orders of Olympias, the wife he had repudiated. No one could guess at the time that his son, reverting to plans which may have been worked out under the influence of certain Greek theoreticians and political thinkers, was to cause an upheaval in the whole structure of the Aegean world and create a new civilization which would spread as far as the shores of the Indus.

4 Athens at the time of Alexander

The period of Athenian history that runs from 336 to 323 B.C. is one about which we are particularly well informed, thanks to the great quantity of documents which have come down to us. Paradoxically, however, historians have tended to neglect this period, losing interest in the sad fate of the city which for almost two centuries had dominated the Aegean world and which the fortunes of war had now reduced to being merely a remote ally of the mighty King of Macedonia, the future conqueror of Asia. To the Greeks of the time, however, the defeat, for all its grave consequences, was an unimportant episode in a long history, and Alexander's adventures did not concern them. They were simply aware that, just as after 404 and again after 355, they must endeavour to tackle immediate difficulties, ensure the city's supplies and resume the efforts made by some of their leaders to develop within the *polis* new activities which the demands of the war against Philip had relegated to the background. The men who directed Athenian policy had realized, by the middle of the century, that hegemony in the Aegean was a thing of the past. Moreover the objective reasons for that hegemony, the threats first from Persia and then from Sparta, had ceased to exist. The Great King had been defeated, driven into the remotest corner of his domain by a conqueror who called himself a Hellene. As for Sparta, she was involved with her own affairs, and was going through a crisis of which the more clear-sighted of her admirers were aware. The task now facing the Athenians was to ensure the provisioning and defence of the city-state (forgetting, if possible, the dread shadow of Macedon) and to provide it with the revenues needed to secure a decent living for every member of the community.

The political climate

Such a project, however, encountered many obstacles, for the men who ruled the state could not be expected to leave the surrounding world totally out of account. The death of Philip, the punishment inflicted on Thebes by Alexander, the desperate endeavour of Agis, King of Sparta, inevitably aroused echoes in Athens, where political passions and personal antagonisms prevailed all the more powerfully in that the chief actors of the preceding period still held the forefront of the stage. But just as had happened twenty years earlier, one man proved able for a few years to impose a consistent policy. His success was all the greater because, although he belonged politically to the tradition of Eubulos, he had given wholehearted support to the policy of Demosthenes in the previous decade and seemed one of the most fervent representatives of the anti-Macedonian party.

The government of Lykourgos Lykourgos was about fifty years old when he was appointed to the post of Treasurer of the Financial Administration. Until then he had played only a minor role. A member of one of the old Athenian families, the Eteoboutades, he had attended Plato's lectures at the Academy and he remained all his life associated with Plato's successor, Xenocrates. His biographer also tells us that he studied under Isokrates in order to train for a political career. He seems to have held no important post before 338 B.C. He is believed, however, to have accompanied Demosthenes and Hypereides on their mission to the Peloponnese in 343, and he unquestionably belonged, like those two famous orators, to the anti-Macedonian party. The course of events did not affect his friendship with both of them, even though he occasionally had to plead against Hypereides in certain lawsuits; but he died before them, and was thus fortunate enough to escape their fate. Immediately after Chaironea, it seems, he was appointed to the extraordinary office which he was to hold for a dozen years, with the title of *tamias epi ten dioi-kesin*.[1] This was the outcome of that tendency which we have already noted to attribute particular importance to the financial administration of the *polis*. In fact, if one is to believe the terms of the decree of Stratokles which, in 307/6, conferred posthumous honour on Lykourgos,[2] it was this financial post which enabled him to exercise almost unlimited control over all the activities of the *polis*.

In the financial field, indeed, the annual revenues of Athens rose to 1200 talents. We may wonder from what sources these were derived. It is usually said that Lykourgos enjoyed the confidence of the rich. It is true that the decree of Stratokles refers to a loan which enabled the *polis*, so short a while after its defeat, to cope with its most urgent expenses. Lykourgos collected 650 talents in this way; but this was an exceptional measure in a particularly critical situation, and it provided an insignificant fraction of the total 18,900 talents which he managed to raise during his twelve years' control of Athens' finances. There can be no doubt, as we shall see later, that the period of Lykourgos' rule coincided with one of great economic activity in Athens: the mines were fully functioning and the *polis* must have drawn substantial profits from them. But it was above all the activity of the port which must have provided Athens with its greatest resources. The number of legal speeches concerning mercantile suits (*dikai emporikai*) that have come down to us is greater for this period than for any other, and this is no accident. Finally, we must not ignore the results of confiscations. Lykourgos, who opened his speech *Against Leokrates* with a eulogy of the system of sycophancy in the interests of the state (3–4), proved a redoubtable adversary to all those on whom his suspicion fell. The writers of antiquity praised his strictness and his austerity, and he never failed to prosecute rich men whose wealth seemed to offer an intolerable challenge. The confiscation of the fortune of Diphilos, a rich mining concession-holder, whom he accused of violating the laws by exploiting columns of ore intended to serve as props for galleries, brought in 160 talents, which were distributed among the people of Athens.

We know too little, unfortunately, about the economic functioning of the Greek world at that time to supply any further details. One fact remains certain: the financial stability which was then the guarantee of economic prosperity, and consequently of the social stability of the *polis*, was achieved during the twelve years that followed Chaironea. As we have seen, part of the revenue thus acquired went to the citizens of Athens; but the larger part was allotted to the reconstitution of the temple treasures, to public building works and to the reorganization of the Athenian army.

Since the Peloponnesian war, in fact, the sanctuaries of the Acropolis had been despoiled of part of the offerings which adorned them.

Out of family piety no doubt, but also in order to restore their former splendour to religious festivals, Lykourgos promoted a number of decrees ordering the restoration of the temple furnishings, in particular of the 'Victories' which had been melted during the last years of the Peloponnesian war, and much equipment for use in processions. To meet the expense of this restoration he set aside the interest on loans granted to individuals on the treasures of the goddess's temple, the rent from sacred lands, and the sale of the skins of sacrificial victims, as well as a subsidy from the city.

The decrees that deal with these various operations[3] are unfortunately too fragmentary to allow one to draw any precise conclusions, but there can be no doubt that by such proceedings Lykourgos was trying to revive the Athens of Perikles. This also explains the policy of public works which was a notable feature of the period. The construction of the Olympeion, which had long been abandoned, was resumed, and work was begun on a new initiation centre (*telesterion*) at Eleusis. It was under Lykourgos that the stone theatre was built at the foot of the Acropolis to replace the old wooden theatre where festivals were held in honour of Dionysos. Other important constructions are also credited to Lykourgos' administration: a gymnasium and a palaestra at the Lyceum, a panathenaic stadium towards the building of which one Eudemos of Plataea offered the state the labour of a yoke of oxen for a thousand days—for which he was rewarded with a crown and the privileges of *isotelia* and *enktesis*, by a decree adopted on the proposal of Lykourgos himself.[4] Athens also owed to Lykourgos the new arsenal at the Piraeus, although work had probably been begun there under the administration of Eubulos. We have the estimates for the construction of this edifice, by the architect Philon: it was a long building of some 120 metres, divided into three longitudinal naves, and serving as warehouse for naval material. The navy stock-lists for this period bear witness to a reconditioning of the ships, of which there were now more than four hundred, and of the sheds which provided shelter for them.[5]

The period of Lykourgos, paradoxically enough at a time when Athens had no foreign policy to speak of, witnessed a reorganization of her military forces. Lykourgos appears to have accumulated on the Acropolis a store of shields and over fifty thousand spears and darts. The fortifications of Athens were reinforced and surrounded by a ditch.[6] Finally, Lykourgos is credited with the reorganization of the *ephebia*, an ancient institution which had fallen into disuse and which aimed at ensuring the defence of the city by a two years' compulsory training of all her young men.[7] It is undoubtedly in connection with this attempt to restore the city's military forces that the functions of the *strategoi* were defined and specialized.

All this, once again, is reminiscent of Periklean Athens. The resemblance, however, is misleading. The Athens whose destinies Lykourgos had taken in hand was not the Athens of the previous century, and we cannot fail to be struck by the notable differences that bespeak a new world. Lykourgos himself was an administrator, not a *strategos* like his illustrious predecessor. The revenues at his disposal came from the city-state, not from subject allies, which explains the stress laid on the defence of Athenian territory, even though the city still had a powerful navy, indispensable for the protection of her trading ships and her supplies. This obviously presupposed a certain economic prosperity: it is not by chance that many decrees were passed during this period in favour of wealthy metics and foreign traders. It also presupposed the continuance of peace, and we can understand why Lykourgos, despite his relentless hostility to Macedon, supported a policy of non-involvement in the disturbances then prevailing throughout the rest of the Hellenic world. When, on the announcement of Philip's death, some Athenians (included Demosthenes) envisaged the possibility of revenge, they had no following. It is significant that Lykourgos was not among those whose extradition was demanded by Alexander after his crushing victory over Thebes, and who were saved at the last minute through the intervention of Phokion. Although these two men were fundamentally opposed in their attitudes towards Macedon, they reacted in the same way—although for different reasons—when confronted with an unrest that could lead nowhere; and it is not by chance that tradition ascribes to both of them the same austerity, the same disdain of wealth.

This, indeed, offers a proof that even after Chaironea the attitude towards Macedon was not the sole principle on which Athenian opinion was divided. It was, however, an essential factor in that division. The period of Lykourgos' government, so fruitful in many ways, was also a time for the settling of accounts between the partisans and adversaries of Macedon, in which Lykourgos himself took part. The only speech of his which has come down to us in its entirety, *Against Leokrates*, although it deals with events subsequent to Chaironea, is not specifically directed against a man of the pro-Macedonian party: Leokrates had fled, he was not in league with Philip. But of the other speeches of which some fragments are extant, two at least, *Against Aristogeiton* and in particular *Against Kephisodotos* were aimed at members of the pro-Macedonian party. The action brought against Aristogeiton was not a political one, even if Demosthenes makes a point of recalling the hostility of Aristogeiton towards Hypereides' project in 338 B.C. But the prosecution of Kephisodotos was in fact directed against Demades, to whom Kephisodotos had proposed to offer exceptional honours for having twice averted Alexander's wrath from Athens. Lykourgos lost his case, and Demades was honoured with a statue on the Agora and the right to dine in the Prytaneion.

The most famous settling of accounts, however, was that between Aeschines and Demosthenes on the subject of the crown which a certain Ktesiphon had proposed to offer the orator for his patriotic share, as Inspector of Works, in the rebuilding of the walls after Chaironea. Ktesiphon's decree was attacked before the Assembly by Aeschines, who brought a *graphe paranomon* against him. The case was not judged until six years later, in 330. This long delay cannot be accounted for solely by the inevitable slowness of the investigation. Possibly the contestants were not anxious to revive old quarrels at a time when the city was in urgent need of relief and recovery. Perhaps Aeschines thought the time was ripe when the failure of the rising of Agis, King of Sparta, might have discredited those who, like Demosthenes, had shown him sympathy. In any case, the lawsuit took place: one of those with which we are best acquainted, since, as with that on the *False Embassy*, we are fortunate enough to have the speeches of both parties. Each of them took the opportunity to justify his own policy and attack that of his adversary. The basis of the affair—the inadmissibility of Ktesiphon's decree—mattered little. What was being judged was the result of twenty years of Athenian policy; and on this point the two speeches provide a document of the highest value. We cannot fail to be struck by the freedom with which the two men express themselves at a time when Alexander, having defeated Darius at Arbeles, was asserting his mastery over the East. This implies that the weight of Macedonian domination was not yet fully felt, and that Alexander's absence in distant parts may have given the Athenians the illusion of freedom. It is, moreover, significant that not only did the judges acquit Ktesiphon, but that

Aeschines did not even win one-fifth of the votes, was condemned to a fine of a thousand drachmas and to partial loss of civic rights, and, judging his political role at an end, chose to leave Athens.

One would hardly be justified, however, in concluding from this verdict that the greater part of Athenian public opinion was in favour of rushing into a fresh adventure. It was probably for reasons quite unconnected with Athenian foreign policy that in 326 Lykourgos, who had twice been re-elected treasurer of the financial administration, was replaced by a certain Menesaichmos, who even brought an action challenging him to render his account. Lykourgos was acquitted; he died soon after, in 324; but his replacement undoubtedly had its political significance. Since 330, in fact, as we shall see later, Athens had been experiencing increased economic difficulties. The extension of the war in Asia had, in particular, adversely affected her grain supplies. It is not impossible that such difficulties may have provoked popular unrest, which some of Lykourgos' opponents may have tried to use against him. Some of them no doubt envisaged the fame to be won through a more active policy, and dreamed of revenge. Others, supporters of Demades and Phokion, were doubtless not sorry to be rid of a man who would not countenance the least concession to those in power. Both groups were to find an opportunity to act with the arrival in Athens of Alexander's paymaster, Harpalos.

The Harpalos affair A great deal of ink has been spilt over this unsavoury affair, not only because the facts themselves are obscure, but above all because the man who had hitherto been in many people's eyes—and in his own—the embodiment of resistance, both patriotic and democratic, to the Macedonian enemy, was to be implicated in it. The facts are known to us chiefly through the speech that Hypereides composed against Demosthenes, and this is the disturbing factor, for if the accusation had come from a member of the pro-Macedonian party it could easily have been written off as a calumny, the verdict of the Areopagus would have been suspect, and the misappropriation of funds, if indeed it had taken place, would have been ascribed to the orator's patriotism; but the presence of Hypereides among the accusers and of Demades among the accused confuses the issue, and embarrasses supporters of the over-simple theory of a straightforward antagonism between pro- and anti-Macedonians.

The affair itself is a complicated one.[8] It was probably at the beginning of 324 B.C., when Alexander returned to Susa, that his paymaster Harpalos absconded with 5,000 talents. This man was no stranger to the Athenians. Two or three years earlier, when famine once again threatened the city, he had sent a cargo of wheat to the Piraeus, earning thereby—like other foreign benefactors of the time—the right of citizenship. Naturally, then, it was in Athens that he sought refuge when, fearing his master's wrath, he decided to leave Asia, taking with him the money for which he was responsible. However, when he came to Athens, he met with some opposition and had to withdraw. Lykourgos had died a short while previously, probably at the beginning of 324, in partial disgrace. Alexander's power was at its apogee and the Athenians may have been unwilling to risk his anger by giving shelter to his fugitive paymaster.

In the political context of the time, it is not surprising that Harpalos was at first coolly received in Athens. Did he, none the less, seek to buy some people's friendship on this occasion? It is not unlikely. A comedy performed at the Great Dionsyia of 324, the *Delos* by Timokles, accuses a number of orators (Hypereides and Demosthenes among them) of accepting bribes. Some might have been activated by their hostility towards the King, others by simple cupidity.

Things were to take quite a different turn with Harpalos' second attempt in May. This time the Athenians consented to receive him, and he settled in Athens, where he lived for some time with the courtesan Pythonike. She died during this brief period, and Harpalos commissioned a statue of his mistress from the sculptor Charikles, who was Phokion's son-in-law.[9] During the month of June an order came from Antipater, in command of the Macedonian forces in Greece, demanding in Alexander's name that Harpalos should be handed over. Phokion opposed this order and, apparently with the consent of Demosthenes, proposed that Harpalos should be kept under guard and his money deposited in the Acropolis. Shortly afterwards Harpalos escaped to Crete, where he was later assassinated, leaving behind in Athens his small daughter by Pythonike, of whom Phokion took charge.

Soon after Harpalos' flight it was realized that half the treasure had disappeared. Obviously all those who had been in contact with the paymaster were suspect, Demosthenes first of all, who had just been appointed to represent Athens at Olympia. He himself demanded that the Areopagus should hold an enquiry into the disappearance of Harpalos' money (early in June 324). Then he left for Olympia, where shortly afterwards Nikanor of Stagyros came with an order from Alexander requiring all Greek cities to recall their exiles.[10] This was of particular concern to Athens, since the implementation of the decree would have resulted in the return of the oligarchs to Samos, and thus constituted a direct threat to the Athenian cleruchs settled there. Demosthenes therefore opposed the carrying out of the decree. On the other hand, after making a formal protest, he had consented to the paying of divine honours to Alexander and the erection of a statue to him in the Agora. Hypereides, in his speech against Demosthenes the following year, did not fail to bring this up against him, and it is true that Demosthenes' behaviour reveals a certain undignified opportunism, which perhaps may have been used to further a consistent policy: it was better to give way over the matter of divine honours and to hold firm over the issue of the exiles.

Demosthenes returned to Athens in October, and soon after, on his instigation, the decision was taken by vote to send an embassy to the King in Babylon. The embassy left in November, taking with it the slaves of Harpalos. Shortly afterwards, at the end of 324 or the beginning of 323, the Areopagus made known the result of its investigation: a number of citizens, including Demosthenes, were accused of having received money from Harpalos and were summoned before an ordinary court. In January and February 323 this court pronounced its verdict. Demosthenes, the first to be judged, was sentenced to a fine of fifty talents. Unable to pay it, he was thrown into prison, but escaped shortly afterwards and took refuge first in Aegina, then in Troezen. The remaining accused were given lighter sentences or even acquitted. Among them was the *strategos* Philokles, whom we hear of again the same year as magistrate in charge (*kosmetes*) of the *epheboi*,[11] Polyeuktes of Sphettos, Aristogeiton (the adversary of Hypereides and Demosthenes in 338), and finally Demades—a heterogeneous group having little in common save venality and the love of money.

This indeed is what Hypereides brings out in his speech against Demosthenes, by whose side he had fought for so many years and whose policy he had constantly upheld:

> You yourself broke up that friendship when you accepted bribes against your country and made a change of front. You made yourself

a laughing-stock and brought disgrace on those who had ever shared your policy in former years. When we might have gained the highest distinction in public life and been accompanied for the remainder of our years by the best of reputations, you frustrated all these hopes, and you are not ashamed, even at your age, to be tried by youths for bribery (*Against Demosthenes*, 21).

In the same speech Hypereides accuses Demosthenes of having loved money for a long time, and of having, on earlier occasions, unhesitatingly appropriated sums entrusted to him by foreign rulers for political ends. Thus the money provided by the Great King to assist the Theban rising was said to have been used by Demosthenes for a shipping loan. We know that the orator's father belonged to that set of rich Athenian 'bourgeois' who increased their wealth by bottomry loans and were thus indirectly involved in commercial affairs. Demosthenes, having recovered his fortune, had followed his father's example. Characteristically, he had a house in the Piraeus, which connected him even more with the mercantile interests of the *polis*. This love of money is not incompatible with the political ambition which he had put to the service of the fight against Macedon; but he was quite capable of appropriating for his own profit part of the money which his various official functions put at his disposal— which was common enough in fourth-century Athens—and furthermore, in certain circumstances, of relegating his ideological principles to the background if they conflicted with his material interests. Hence his support of a certain kind of pacifism, and his acceptance of a situation which a man of greater integrity, such as Hypereides, who incidentally was protected from such temptations, being a wealthy landowner of traditional type, refused to accept.

We must not attempt, as some have done, to make excuses for Demosthenes, to explain the 'deduction in advance' of twenty talents of which he was held guilty, as a patriotic act in the interests of his country's revenge, and the verdict of the Areopagus, followed by that of the people's court, as 'the result of a political manoeuvre against Demosthenes'. [12] Or rather we must interpret the whole affair, of which Harpalos' money was the pretext, as a reflection of the troubled state of Athenian public opinion. For a long time the Athenians had been under the illusion that nothing had changed and that in spite of a few upheavals, severely repressed, the Greece of the city-states, relieved of the struggle for hegemony, was about to enjoy a period of peace in which she could profitably pursue commercial activities. The lean years 330–327, the increased difficulties of supply, the weight of Alexander's power, felt more threateningly as he returned into Western Asia, had shattered this fine optimism. Some Athenians dreaded a renewal of warfare and felt the need for extreme prudence; others, on the contrary, hoped for a reawakening of Greece. Lykourgos, who dreamed of an impossible revival of Athenian greatness, in peace and independence, was as far removed from one group as from the other. Hence his failure to be re-elected in 326 and the increasing mistrust felt of him by his fellow-citizens.

Phokion and the men of the Macedonian party favoured the policy of prudence, but they were supported by all those who feared lest a war-mongering policy should jeopardize the fruits of Lykourgos' wise administration, that is to say by the mass of the well-to-do, by all those who had grown rich by exploiting mines or financing shipping. Demosthenes was one of these, and, while maintaining his characteristic attitude, was prepared to make a good many concessions. As for Hypereides, he represented those who remained loyal to their past and were ready to undertake any wild venture for its own sake, while nevertheless putting up with the existing situation, which distressed them only by contrast with their old ideal—the perennial type of 'committed' intellectual. Behind Hypereides and his friends were a host of men who hoped for material advantage from a war of revenge, and, needless to say, the mass of the *demos*. We can thus understand why Demosthenes suffered the severest penalty; more than Demades or Aristogeiton, he seemed a traitor to the people's cause and, as such, deserved to be more harshly punished than the others.

The Harpalos affair thus finds a place in the political history of Athenian democracy in its decline, and reveals the contradictions within that democracy. Originally a banal incident devoid of immediate significance, it reflects the political atmosphere that prevailed in Athens on the eve of the Lamian war.

The economic and financial crisis: food shortage and rising prices

The political atmosphere was the result of the crisis which the city-state had been undergoing since 330 B.C. This deserves further study. We have already seen that since 355, when Athens renounced imperialism, there had been a remarkable upswing of economic life. This was shown in particular in the vigorous revival of mining activity and in the development of Athenian trade, to which the progress of commercial and banking techniques and the multiplicity of commercial undertakings bear witness. The defeat of 338 did not, for the time being, slow down this activity. Most of those speeches in the Demosthenean *corpus* which deal with commercial affairs date from the years 340–330. They bring to life a picturesque and colourful business world: the traders include many foreigners, men from Marseilles (*Against Zenothemis*), Phaselites, Egyptians and so forth, having correspondents in Pontus (*Against Phormion*), in Syracuse, in Egypt, that is to say in all the markets where traders from Athens replenished their store of grain. Merchants and ship-builders formed associations, more or less provisional, which were often dissolved at the end of a particular operation but which sometimes lasted longer. As for the money-lenders, they were frequently, as we have seen, rich citizens who by this means played a part in the commercial life of the *polis* and thereby came to form close relations with foreigners. The speeches, of course, tell us about the affairs that turned out badly. But there were many others which succeeded and enabled rich men to become even richer. We have seen that Hypereides reproached Demosthenes with being one of these. What chiefly strikes one is the coexistence of citizens and foreigners among the money-lenders, who now formed a single class of businessmen, liable to be judged by the same courts, having the same interests at stake; and the 'political' difference between them tended to diminish. It was no accident that during this period a large number of decrees were passed conferring honours on wealthy foreigners who took advantage of Athens' difficulties of supply to display their generosity towards the city. We must note that such honours often included the more concrete privilege of *enktesis*, the right to acquire land in Attica. Thus, under cover of the development of trade, new social relations grew up which were in contradiction with the traditional ethic of the *polis*.

However, although defeat failed to slow down activity in the Piraeus, at any rate during the first years after Chaironea, while on the contrary Lykourgos' policy attracted all those who practised barter in the Mediterranean—the figure of 10,000 metics given in 317 in the census taken by Demetrios of Phaleron is significant—the fact remains that after 330 things changed. To what must we attribute the difficulties of supply experienced by the city-state at that time, which caused a rise in the price of agricultural products in particular? [13]

Several hypotheses have been put forward. It is certain that Alexander's expedition deflected considerable resources towards the East, and that the large amount of money put into circulation by the conqueror must inevitably have had repercussions on the Mediterranean market, about which we still know very little. But the crisis cannot be explained solely by economic causes. The speech against Phormion, which was made in the early days of this crisis, refers to the difficulties encountered by a trader who left Athens with a cargo and who failed to sell his merchandise in the Bosphoros on account of the war that King Perisades was then being forced to wage against the Scythians. [14] This same speech implicates a certain Lampis who, starting from Athens, bought wheat in the Bosphoros and sold it at Akanthos, in Chalkidike, while at that very time there was a shortage of wheat in Athens. [15] The same accusation is made in the speech *Against Dionysodoros*: a certain Parmeniskos, having sailed from Athens with a ship and money borrowed in Athens from the plaintiff and his associate, shipped a load of wheat to Egypt, but having been warned by his correspondent that the price of wheat had dropped in Athens following the arrival of a consignment of Sicilian wheat he unloaded his cargo at Rhodes. [16]

This story suggests a number of comments. Firstly, we cannot fail to be struck by the existence of networks of information enabling traders to speculate on the price of wheat and unload their cargo where prices were most favourable. Secondly, we can gauge the primitive character of economic processes, since a single consignment of wheat from Sicily was enough to make prices drop so markedly. Furthermore, these two examples bear witness to the unquestionable decline of Athenian power, for it is obvious that, in the days when Athens dominated the Aegean, traders sailing from Athens would not have dared infringe the law which ordered them to bring back the whole or part of their cargo to that city. We cannot doubt that if between 330 and 323 Athens repeatedly experienced a serious shortage of grain, it was because the cases of Lampis and Parmeniskos were by no means exceptional. Moreover, we should not be misled by the benefactions of certain rich foreigners; traders by sea tended increasingly to desert the city for more profitable places, among which Rhodes occupied a privileged position.

Did the crisis which affected Athenian trade also affect other aspects of economic life, as has been suggested? The answer is hard to formulate, since we lack sufficient data for an assessment. We have already seen that one result of Lykourgos' policy had been to revive certain industries, such as public building works and arsenals. Athenian craftsmanship still flourished, and the ceramic industry was to yield much fine work; but this was a traditional activity which played only a minor part in the economic life of the *polis*.

The mines were a different matter. We have seen how, from 355 onwards, they too enjoyed a definite revival, to which the inscriptions of *poletai* and the speeches in lawsuits bear witness, as well as the most recent excavations on the Thorikos site. This revival proved profitable chiefly to the concession-holders, who belonged to the wealthy class and were also well known as landowners, *strategoi* or trierarchs. If we confine ourselves to the evidence of the lists of the *poletai*, it appears to have been short-lived, and here too a decline is evident after 330. We must, however, avoid the temptation to connect the decline of mining activities with the commercial crisis in Athens. In point of fact, and notwithstanding the complaints of the orator in the speech *Against Phainippos*, the mining industry seems to have been still prosperous in Athens in the last quarter of the fourth century, and in any case to have given scope for the accumulation of large fortunes such as those to which Hypereides alludes in his speech *For Euxenippos* (43–4). The misfortunes of the mining industry to which the opponent of Phainippos refers [17] may well have been connected with Lykourgos' efforts at reorganization and with the actions brought against dishonest concessionaries, rather than with any side-effects of Alexander's conquests or the introduction of Persian gold into the money market. This does not mean that these lawsuits did not have adverse effects on the mining industry; the wealthy classes grew apprehensive, and were reluctant to invest their capital in the mines (Hypereides' speech *For Euxenippos* refers to their anxiety).

Political reasons are therefore not to be ignored. Other more complex reasons may perhaps be added to them, which concern economics as well as politics. The speech against Phainippos, even allowing for the orator's exaggeration, does reveal the existence of a certain opposition between 'landowners' and those involved in industry—*hoi georgountes* and *hoi en tois ergois ergazomenoi*.

We have already had occasion to note that these two categories were not mutually exclusive. A rich man in fourth-century Athens could be a landed proprietor and at the same time the owner of one or more mining concessions or factories, increasing his wealth meanwhile by bottomry loans. But in so far as these different activities had become equally remunerative, and both contributed to the production of wealth, we can understand how some men devoted all their efforts to some particular branch of economic activity, conceived of precisely as such and no longer merely as the normal source of income of a respectable citizen. Demosthenes' father, in the first half of the fourth century, had been an Athenian 'bourgeois' living on the income from his workshops and quite prepared to advance money in bottomry loans. He was, strictly speaking, engaged neither in trade nor in industry, any more than his son could be described as a trader when he misappropriated the sums entrusted to him in order to finance a shipping loan. But the prosecutor in the speech *Against Phainippos* speaks as a representative of industry, and in that capacity, with never a hint of the aristocratic ethical code that still found expression in Aristophanes, takes up his stand against the landed proprietor who speculates on the selling price of agricultural products. Similarly, the mining concession-holders referred to by Hypereides in the speech *For Euxenippos* represented industry, and they made considerable profits, since the fortune of one of them was reckoned at 60 talents, while Epikrates of Pallenaea and his associates made 300 talents from the concession they had been exploiting together for three years.

On the other hand, Phainippos was no simple farmer living on the produce of his estate. He was a cultivator of the land, owning a vast estate and deriving substantial profit from it. True, the prosecutor only gives us incomplete information, which does not entitle us to draw any general conclusions. Even the extent of the estate is only vaguely indicated, and this has allowed modern scholars to indulge in every sort of calculation in an effort to define it precisely.[18] The generally accepted figure of 300 hectares has recently been challenged; but even if reduced to 50 or 60 hectares, Phainippos' estate was still very large. Now his adversary implies that he was not alone in speculating on the price of agricultural produce and drawing profit from his cultivation: 'men of wealth . . . who produce large quantities of grain and wine and dispose of this at three times its former price' (*Against Phainippos*, 31). As L. Gernet has pointed out in his introduction to the speech *Against Phainippos*,[19] one really has the impression of a sort of 'class jealousy' between those who drew their wealth from mining and the agriculturalists, the latter being accused of 'enjoying shocking prosperity'.

What real basis is there for these accusations? One must undoubtedly allow for the prosecutor's bias; but it is not impossible that the years 330–320 were prosperous ones for landowners. The difficulties of provisioning Athens allowed them to speculate on the price of agricultural produce. Phainippos was able in one year to make 3 talents from the sale of his wheat and barley, and nearly 2 talents from the sale of his wine, not to mention that of his wood, which brought him in 20 drachmas a day. His case was obviously not exceptional; the prosecutor's arguments must have been plausible to convince the judges. We see the implications clearly: on the one hand, that agriculture was no longer just an ideal pastime for gentlefolk, as in the days when Xenophon wrote his *Oeconomicus*, but a profitable occupation on a level with the mining industry; on the other hand, that large estates like that of Phainippos were not exceptional. On this point, however, we have to admit ignorance. For this period we have practically no figures and have, therefore, to argue from extremely fragmentary data.

Certain facts stand out. There was an increase in the number of political trials in Athens after 356, in that somewhat disturbed atmosphere that prevailed during the conflict with Philip. The penalties imposed at these trials generally included confiscation of property, often of landed property. Estates thus changed hands more and more frequently, and it is most likely that many of those who bought the properties put up for sale were already landowners themselves. Besides these confiscated properties, public lands were sometimes sold by the state. Between 340 and 320 such sales took place, as we know from inscriptions.[20] One may question the causes of these sales, perhaps connected with the difficulty of finding farmers in the existing political situation; but here again, although the portions of land sold were relatively small, we may assume that the purchasers were already landowners.

One final comment must be made: in his *Ways and Means*, Xenophon noted that 'when corn and wine are abundant, the crops are cheap and the profit derived from them disappears; so that many give up farming and set up as merchants or shopkeepers or moneylenders' (IV). May we not suppose that the rise in the price of wheat and wine produced the contrary phenomenon, and that rich

landowners, who had taken up mining concessions, decided not to renew them in view of the risks involved in the mining industry, but to
acquire landed property instead ? This has been suggested, in fact, to
explain the slowing-down of mining activity after 330.²¹ One must of
course avoid drawing hasty conclusions; but we may assume that
men who had developed a taste for money may have been capable of
following this line of reasoning, preferring the reliable profitability
of real estate to the uncertain gains to be made from mine-working.

It goes without saying, once again, that only the rich, or relatively
well-to-do, were involved. For the small peasant, capable only of
providing for his own needs, the rise in the price of agricultural
produce brought no advantages, particularly as that rise did not
affect all such produce but primarily wheat and wine. Now the small
peasant in Attica was often obliged to buy his flour, while the few
vegetables he could sell in the market brought in scarcely anything.
All this only intensified his poverty. Of the latter we have no
directly contemporary evidence, but when, after the Lamian war, the
victor, Antipater, imposed a system of restricted franchise, ten
thousand Athenians, deprived of citizenship, were to emigrate into
Thrace, where they had been offered land by the Macedonian ruler.
This surely proves an increase in peasant poverty in the years
preceding the Lamian war.

There can be no doubt that from 330 onwards Athens experienced
grave economic difficulties. The revival of economic life which had
characterized the forties of the fourth century was still going on; but
on the one hand it came into conflict with traditional structures
which were still very powerful, and on the other it presupposed an
extension of the barter system which was precluded by Alexander's
campaign in Asia. Hence this apparently paradoxical result: whereas
since the sixth century the prosperity of Athens depended essentially
on the development of her craftsmanship and on trade, of which the
Piraeus was the centre, it was agriculture, particularly the cultivation
of cereals, which on the eve of her last spasmodic attempt to safeguard her liberty constituted her most profitable economic activity.

The Lamian war

Leosthenes perceived that the whole of Greece was humiliated and
cowed, corrupted by men who were accepting bribes from Philip and

Alexander against their native countries. He realized that our city
stood in need of a commander, and Greece herself of a city, able
to assume the leadership, and he gave himself to his country
and the city to the Greeks, in the cause of freedom (*Funeral
Speech*, 10).

This passage of Hypereides' funeral speech in honour of those who
fell during the first year of the Lamian war is revealing of the frame
of mind of a whole section of Athenian public opinion. For such men
the Macedonian alliance was a fraud; the entire world was forced to
obey a single master, and the ancestral laws were flouted. They saw
'. . . sacrifices being made to men; images, altars and temples care-
fully perfected in their honour, while those of the gods are neglected,
and we ourselves are forced to honour as heroes the servants of these
people' (ibid. 21). Alexander's latest decrees, and the eagerness with
which some people submitted to them, brought out the more clearly
the deceptive character of the Hellenic League. Athens alone could
lead a movement of resistance in the name of Greek liberty. For this
there was needed—and the fact is significant—a man of sufficient
stature to assume the leadership. Undoubtedly Hypereides did not
feel equal to it. He was too old, for one thing—he was about 67 in
323 B.C.—and above all he was an Assembly man rather than a man
of action. Now it is by no means certain that the Assembly would
have followed him if, prior to the death of Alexander, he had proposed open hostilities against Macedon. The fear of new financial
burdens would have aroused the opposition of the rich, and the mass
of the people were not prepared to launch out into operations whose
issues may have seemed dubious and which at first sight appeared
unnecessary. He himself, in the *Funeral Speech*, does not seek to
conceal the fact that the initiative came from Leosthenes.

It is important, therefore, to consider the problems that arise in
connection with Leosthenes, and his share of responsibility for the
outbreak of the Lamian war. Since the discovery of the Oropos
inscription, it is generally accepted that Leosthenes was the son of
the *strategos* of the same name who, having been impeached after his
defeat at Peparethos, had fled from Athens in 361 and taken refuge
with Philip.[22] Like other Athenian *strategoi*, victims of factional
conflict during those troubled years of the mid fourth century, he had
become leader of a band of stateless mercenaries. His son, born in
exile and deprived of his property, had an adventurous youth.

Circumstances were then particularly favourable for a professional soldier's existence. He had served in Asia, and like other Greek mercenaries had come to adopt an increasingly hostile attitude towards Alexander. At the beginning of 324 he was at Cape Tenares with the mercenaries who had been sent back from Asia by their generals, on orders from Alexander, and this young military chief already enjoyed such prestige among his men that they appointed him *strategos autokrator*, possibly to replace another Athenian, condemned like himself to the life of an exiled mercenary leader—the famous Chares, friend of Demosthenes and Hypereides, who must have died about that time. There is no doubt that Chares, while leading an adventurer's life, had kept up political contacts with Athens, and he may have provided the link between the orator and the young military leader. At all events, when Leosthenes returned to Athens he was elected territorial *strategos* for the year 324/3. There is nothing surprising about this situation, which had become quite common in the second half of the fourth century, and which reflects the evolution of institutions, particularly of the office of *strategos*. It is highly probable that Hypereides had ulterior motives when he supported the election of Leosthenes to this post. But, as Ettore Lepore has shown in an article in *La Parola del Passato*, the military and diplomatic preparations for the Lamian war took place outside the political framework of the *polis*; it seems, indeed, that even before the death of Alexander Leosthenes had made sure of an alliance with the peoples of Central Greece, particularly with the Aitolians.[23]

The news of the conqueror's death inevitably brought things to a head. Plutarch, in the *Life of Phokion* (22), describes the agitation that prevailed in Athens when the announcement came. For Leosthenes and for Hypereides, this was the opportunity to get the state to ratify a decision which had been taken without its knowledge, giving a political character to what had begun as a mercenaries' revolt. After a debate, the Assembly voted officially for war, and Leosthenes was put in command of operations, while the hoplites were mobilized and an amnesty proclaimed, which enabled Demosthenes to return to Athens. Undoubtedly his policy, up till the death of Alexander, had been akin to that supported by Phokion: one of abstention from any sort of political adventure. But Demosthenes' exile, then the death of the King and the excitement that seized Athens on the news of it, suddenly restored a meaning to the war. It seemed that Athens had once again become the leader of a united Greece in defence of liberty.

The first victories won by Leosthenes seemed to justify Hypereides and his political friends in their choice. While Leosthenes advanced towards Thermopylai, occupying 'the pass through which in bygone days as well, the barbarians marched against the Greeks' (*Funeral Speech*, 12), the army of Athenian hoplites, having defeated the Macedonian garrison in the Kadmea, joined up with Leosthenes' mercenaries, and after a victorious battle against Antipater's troops in the neighbourhood of Trachinian Heraklea forced the Macedonian general to withdraw to Lamia. The siege of Lamia lasted throughout the winter of 323/2 B.C.; during a sortie, Leosthenes was killed by a missile from a sling. The death of the *strategos* did not bring an end to operations. His successor, Antiphilos, however, was forced to raise the siege on learning of the arrival of a relieving force under Leonnatos. Leonnatos was defeated and killed in a battle fought in the spring of 322; and it was soon after this that Hypereides delivered his funeral speech, from which it is clear that in Athens victory then seemed as good as won: 'For who could rightly grudge his praise to those of our citizens who fell in this campaign, who gave their lives for the freedom of the Greeks, convinced that the surest proof of their desire to guarantee the liberty of Greece was to die in battle for her?' (*Funeral Speech*, 16).

The Athenians, however, were reckoning without the reality of Macedon's military might; thanks to the reinforcements brought up by Krateros, in August or September 322 Antipater crushed the Greek army at Krannon.

> The Greeks were defeated. Their defeat was not severe, nor did many of them fall, but owing to their lack of obedience to their commanders, who were young and soft-hearted, and because at the same time Antipater made tempting overtures to their several cities, their army melted away and most shamefully abandoned the cause of freedom (*Life of Phokion*, 26).

We may give credence to these remarks of Plutarch's, even if we interpret them in a way the moralist had not foreseen. It is indubitable, indeed, that the war had been a hasty and reckless venture, that it did not reflect any consistent policy, and that since the death of Leosthenes there was lacking that absolute authority which alone could have held together such disparate elements as the mercenaries from Cape Tenares, the Athenian hoplites, the Thessalian horsemen and the rest.

In Athens, now as in 338, the fear of seeing the city occupied by the enemy favoured the negotiations undertaken by those who had not fully shared the warlike enthusiasm of Hypereides and his friends. One of the leaders of this group was obviously Phokion, who, relying on support from the contacts he had in Antipater's entourage, undertook to lead the negotiations.

The conditions imposed on the Athenians were extremely harsh. They must hand over Demosthenes and Hypereides, restore a system of restricted franchise, accept a Macedonian garrison at Munychia and shoulder the whole cost of the war, plus compensation. Phokion made an attempt to get the Macedonian garrison withdrawn, since this symbolized the loss of freedom for Athens and justified, *a posteriori*, those who had started the war in the name of Greek liberty. Antipater refused, however, arguing that this garrison would provide Phokion with the surest guarantee that order would be maintained.[24]

We can imagine the reaction of the Athenian *demos* to the announcement of such conditions. Plutarch tells us that the adoption of the new constitution disfranchised some 12,000 persons.[25] Diodoros gives a higher figure, stating that out of 30,000 Athenians only 9,000 retained their citizenship,[26] the other 21,000 being deprived of civic rights. These were obviously the poorest citizens, those whose fortune amounted to less than 2,000 drachmas. Antipater offered them land in Thrace, and according to Diodoros 10,000 of them accepted exile; but the rest, who stayed at home, were clearly in a lamentable and humiliating position (cf. *Life of Phokion*, 28). These men had formed the *demos* of Athens, and only a short while previously had held control of the city's fate. It is understandable that it needed the presence of a Macedonian garrison to make them accept the loss of their citizenship and all the material advantages that went with it, and that Phokion made no great efforts to persuade Antipater to withdraw this garrison, particularly since his friend Menyllos had been put in charge of it. The situation, however, was tense enough to cause unease and discontent even among those wealthy Athenians who had retained their citizenship, and it was to have its repercussions when the death of Antipater ushered in a period of crisis in Greece.

As for Demosthenes and Hypereides, who had fled from Athens

on hearing the news of the defeat, they were to die within a few days of one another, Demosthenes by taking poison in the temple of Poseidon at Kalauria, Hypereides after being captured and tortured before the eyes of Antipater, at Kleones. As each of them had fore-seen, Greek liberty and the greatness of Athens were at an end.

5 The period of Diadochoi

The period that opens in 322 B.C. is one of the most complex in the whole history of the Aegean world.[1] The death of Alexander and the lack of an heir capable of succeeding him and holding his empire together were to result in those conflicts between *diadochoi* which were to end only forty-two years later with the stabilization of the great Hellenistic monarchies and the division of the empire between the descendants of Ptolemy, Seleukos and Antigonos.

In this vast maelstrom, where everything was decided by force of arms, Athens could play but a minimal part. Strictly watched by a Macedonian garrison, she was incapable of independent action. Yet the illusions of the men who governed her and the prestige which she still enjoyed were to make of her, oddly enough, if not a crucial factor, at any rate an important stake in the contest between Alexander's generals. She was also to be, during the last quarter of the fourth century, the scene of an experiment in 'philosophical tyranny' and the home of the most brilliant 'epigones', while schools of philosophy flourished and the New Comedy, with Menander, expressed the realities of a society very different from the civic community of old.[2]

The 'philosophical tyranny' of Demetrios of Phaleron [3]

We have seen earlier how Antipater, on his victory, imposed on the Athenians an oligarchic constitution and the presence of a Macedonian garrison at Munychia, and how, fearing unrest and disorder, those who then controlled the destinies of Athens, Phokion in particular, had bowed before the Macedonian demands.

The death of Antipater brought about a marked alteration. The old regent, who shortly before his death had assumed the title of *epimeletes* of the Kings, had chosen to succeed him Polyperchon, a veteran officer of Philip's, instead of his own son Kassander. A coalition was formed against the new regent in which Kassander was joined by the masters of Alexander's former empire, Lysimachos, Antigonos and Ptolemy. Polyperchon, his back to the wall, sought support from the Greek city-states, which were still a force to be reckoned with, and in particular from Athens. In an edict recorded by Diodoros[4] he proclaimed, in the name of the Kings, an amnesty for past offences and a return to the situation that preceded the Lamian war. This meant the abandonment of the oligarchic constitution, but not a restoration of independence, since there was no question of withdrawing the Munychia garrison, particularly as Kassander, in order to take Polyperchon by surprise, had promptly sent Nikanor to the Piraeus with orders to hold on in Munychia. The presence of the Macedonian garrison did not prevent the Athenians from meeting in an Assembly to proclaim the restoration of democracy:

> The Athenian people, meeting together in an assembly, dismissed its former magistrates, replaced them by the most fervent democrats and condemned all those who had participated in the oligarchic government, some to death and others to banishment with loss of property. Among the latter was Phokion . . . (Diodoros XVIII, 65).

Plutarch in his *Life of Phokion* gives a far more detailed account of these events. He declares that immediately on the death of Antipater Phokion gave his support to Kassander and facilitated Nikanor's entry into the Piraeus. When Polyperchon's decision became known, there was great excitement among the Athenians, who now turned against Phokion. 'A disorderly and informal assembly', comprising aliens, disfranchised persons and exiles who had returned with Polyperchon's son Alexander, was held; Phokion was dismissed from his office and new *strategoi* were appointed. Two embassies were then sent to Polyperchon, one led by Phokion and the other by the democratic orator Hagnonides. The audience, held in presence of the King, Philip, took place in a disturbed and almost farcical atmosphere, and finally Phokion was brought back to Athens as a prisoner to be judged there, together with those who had accompanied him. Plutarch tells us:

> The manner of their return to the city was shameful, for they were carried on waggons through the Kerameikos to the theatre. For

thither Kleitos brought them and there he kept them, until the
magistrates had made up an assembly, from which they excluded
neither slave, foreigner, nor disfranchised person, but allowed all
alike, both men and women, free access to the theatre and tribunal.
After the letter of the King had been read aloud, in which he said
that according to his judgement the men were traitors, but that their
fellow-citizens, who were freemen and self-governing, should pro-
nounce sentence upon them, Kleitos led the men in (*Life of Phokion*,
34).

In a tumultuous atmosphere the decree proposed by Hagnonides,
demanding the death penalty for all the accused, was approved; and
'when the show of hands was taken, no one keeping his seat, but all
rising to their feet, and most of them wreathing themselves with
garlands, they condemned the men to death' (ibid. 35).

The procedure was unquestionably illegal, and recalled the trial of
the Argusinae; but its illegality was increased by the fact that aliens
and slaves were present in the Assembly. Are we to give credence to
Plutarch's statement? Its implications are obvious. For while there
can be no doubt that some Athenians who had been disfranchised in
322 took part in the Assembly, it seems harder to credit that only
four years later men who were not members of the citizen body, and
in particular slaves, could have got in among the Athenians by fraud.
We shall have to admit that if Plutarch's assertion is well founded,
the Athenian *demos* must have countenanced the presence in its ranks
of slaves, aliens and even women. This reveals the extent to which
the traditional ideal of the *polis* had altered in a few years.

The democracy thus restored was not to be long-lived. Less than a
year later, Kassander had become master of the Piraeus, which
meant that Athens' supplies were completely cut off, and the
Athenians were forced to come to terms with him. The Macedonian
insisted on the maintenance of a garrison in Munychia and the
return to an oligarchic constitution, although a more moderate one
than that established five years earlier by Antipater, the census rate
being fixed at ten *minai*. Furthermore, the supreme authority was to
be vested in a man whom Kassander trusted: the philosopher and
orator Demetrios of Phaleron. He had been condemned to death
with Phokion in 318; but having been out of Athens at that time, he
had avoided his sentence, and had taken refuge with Kassander,
with whom he had become friends. He was a good orator and a

cultured man, who had studied under Theophrastos, Aristotle's successor at the head of the Peripatetic school. He was about thirty at the time, and he was to rule Athens with absolute authority for ten years. Plutarch, in the *Life of Demetrios* (10), observes that the regime over which Demetrios of Phaleron presided was aristocratic in name and monarchic in fact.

The problem is to ascertain by what constitutional expedient this absolute authority was exercised. Ancient sources give Demetrios at least three different titles: Polybios (XII, xiii, 9) describes him as *prostates*, protector or patron of the *polis*, Strabo (IX, 98) and Diodoros (XX, xlv, 5) call him *epistates*, possibly by analogy with the title borne in the third century by the representatives of Hellenistic kings in the city-states subject to those kings, but elsewhere Diodoros always uses the vaguer term *epimeletes* (XVIII, lxxiv, 3 and XX, xlv, 2), particularly when reporting the terms of the treaty concluded with Kassander. This last term is presumably the only correct one, especially as it has equivalents elsewhere. It was as *epimeletes* that Hieronymos of Kardia governed Thebes, and two years later Kassander appointed an *epimeletes* as governor of Megalopolis. But both these terms, *epimeletes* and *epistates*, refer chiefly to the functions performed by Demetrios in relation to Kassander. It is therefore important to determine what these functions were within the framework of the Athenian constitution. An inscription of 315/14 B.C. (*Syll.*[3] 319, 1.9–11) provides important information about this. Demetrios was then acting as *strategos* for the fourth time. This means that he governed the city with that title as soon as he took power; and it can be assumed that, like Perikles or Phokion, he got himself re-elected regularly each year, except perhaps in 309/8 when he appears in the list of archons. We cannot fail to note the fact: the political reaction represented by the government of Demetrios was reflected in the institutional sphere by a return to ancient customs, to the plurality of civil and military functions in the hands of certain *strategoi*.

This absolute authority was used by Demetrios in the service of a policy of reform in which we trace the influence of the Peripatetic school. We have already seen that Kassander imposed on the Athenians a regime of restricted franchise whereby citizenship was confined to the possessors of a fortune of at least ten *minai*. It was no doubt in order to be able to establish the new list of those with full civic rights that Demetrios undertook the famous census, the results of which are reported by Ktesikles (ap. Ath. VI, 272b): Athens was said to have comprised 21,000 citizens, 10,000 metics and 400,000 slaves. The last figure, which some have considered too high, has been the subject of much discussion (see below, page 117). What must be chiefly noted is that despite the adoption of a regime of restricted franchise, the basis of Athenian democracy remained relatively broad, and we cannot fail to recognize here the imprint of Aristotelian teaching. The reduction of the rate to half that established in 322 meant a decrease in the number of disfranchised persons (*atimoi*), who, as the events of 318 had shown, could be a serious source of disturbance. Other constitutional provisions give further evidence of Aristotelian influence: magistrates were to be appointed by election rather than by lot, and subjected to closer surveillance, being required to render their accounts twice a month before the *Boule*, while a college of seven *nomophylachi*, guardians of the laws, was created to preside over the sessions of the Assembly and ensure that the laws were respected. We may also assume that state-pay (*misthophoria*) was suppressed, although we have no proof of this.

Ancient sources dwell on the financial stability enjoyed by Athens during the ten years of Demetrios' government. This can be accounted for by the continuance of peace and the suppression of *misthoi* and of the *theorikon*. The war fleet had been reduced to twenty ships by the treaty with Kassander. The presence of a Macedonian garrison in Munychia relieved Demetrios of the need to resort to mercenaries. The revenues of the *polis* were thus no longer swallowed up by military expenses. Meanwhile the mines were being worked, and the Piraeus was still a focus of activity. We can understand how it became possible for the state to undertake the organization of choruses and the preparation of competitions, in particular of the Dionysiac competitions for which a special magistrate, the *agonothetes*, was elected each year. Here again we glimpse a development which altered the traditional ideal of the *polis* and which heralds the Hellenistic epoch.

A final aspect of Demetrios' policy is the one which ancient writers stressed particularly. This disciple of Theophrastos, who in fact had a certain liking for display and whose private life was far from exemplary, professed to be a strict moralist and imposed on the city a series of sumptuary laws, limiting expenditure on funerals and monuments, reviving certain long-forgotten laws of Solon, instituting a body of magistrates, the *gynaikonomoi*, whose special function was to apply the laws restricting luxury in women's dress. These measures were clearly not dictated solely by the desire to remain faithful to the principles of the Peripatetic school; they enabled Demetrios to allay the resentment of the majority against a luxury which had become more blatant during the course of the century. We recognize a certain demagogic element in his policy. The historian Demochares, nephew of Demosthenes, accused Demetrios of being concerned chiefly with giving material satisfaction to the *demos*. Polybios reports the indictment:

> Demochares in his history brings accusations by no means trivial against Demetrios, telling us that . . . his boast had been that the market in the town was plentifully supplied and cheap, and that there was abundance of all the necessities of life for everybody. He tells us that a snail moved by machinery went in front of his procession, spitting out saliva, and that donkeys were marched through the theatre, to show, forsooth, that the country had yielded up to others all the glory of Greece and obeyed the behests of Kassander. Of all this, he says, he was in no wise ashamed (XII, 13).

Bread and circuses—at all events this policy enjoyed the support of a section of the *demos*, for calm seems to have prevailed in Athens during the ten years of Demetrios' government, while the Athenians passed decrees in his honour and raised statues to him.

There existed none the less an opposing group, who looked increasingly towards one of the *diadochoi* whose prestige appeared to be growing, Antigonos the One-eyed.[5] He had gained control of Lemnos and Imbros, welcomed by the Athenian cleruchs whom his promises had seduced. His defeat at Gaza in 312 was, however, to destroy for a while the hopes that Athenian 'democrats' had fastened on him. In 311 Antigonos concluded a peace with Kassander, Lysimachos and Ptolemy which reasserted the right to autonomy of the Greek city-states, a right which was purely fictitious since none of the four men intended to relinquish control over the cities in the area under his authority. Antigonos, however, appears to have used the proclamation of 311 as an instrument of propaganda, as appears from his letter to the people of Skepsis in Troas (*OGI S*, 5 = Welles, No. 1). It is not surprising, therefore, that when, encouraged by the success of Antigonos, his son Demetrios Poliorketes appeared before Athens at the head of a fleet of 250 ships, he immediately found supporters. Demetrios of Phaleron fled, while democracy was restored in Athens.

> The Athenians, Stratokles writing the decree, voted to set up statues of Antigonos and Demetrios in a chariot near the statues of Harmodius and Aristogeiton, to give them both honorary crowns at a cost of two hundred talents, to consecrate an altar to them and call it the altar of the Saviours, to add to the ten tribes two more, Demetrias and Antigonis, to hold annual games in their honour with a procession and a sacrifice, and to weave their portraits in the peplos of Athena. Thus the common people, deprived of power in the Lamian war by Antipater, fifteen years afterwards unexpectedly recovered the constitution of their fathers (Diodoros XX, 46).

The philosophical tyranny of Demetrios of Phaleron had been only a brief halt in the irremediable decadence of the *polis*. The democracy restored by Demetrios Poliorketes was a mere caricature of the regime which had constituted the greatness of Athens.

Demetrios Poliorketes, master of Athens

The domination of Demetrios Poliorketes over Athens was to last for six years, from June 307 until the battle of Ipsos.

As a matter of fact the Macedonian did not reside regularly in Athens during these six years. As early as the spring of 306 he had returned to the Aegean on a summons from his father, who was preparing to attack Ptolemy. He came back to Athens only at the end of 304 and spent the winter there. Then, on several occasions, during his conflict with Kassander, he intervened in Athenian affairs. The term 'domination' must therefore be qualified, and the first problem facing the historian is to discover in what ways the son of Antigonos imposed his authority on the Athenians.

Formally, as we have seen, democracy had been restored and the independence of the city-state proclaimed. This implied, on the one hand, the abandonment of the regime of restricted franchise imposed by Kassander and the restitution of political rights to those who had been deprived of them in 317, and on the other the complete restoration of traditional democratic institutions. However, we must not delude ourselves. These institutions had undergone a profound upheaval during the last fifteen years, and it seems that the more clear-sighted democratic leaders understood the need for a complete revision of the laws, to which end a college of *nomothetes* was appointed.

In other respects, it is quite clear that this neo-democracy was to preserve certain new institutions which had made their appearance during the last decades of the century, such as the office of Treasurer of the general administration, which was entrusted in 307/6 to the son of Lykourgos, Habron. The addition of two new tribes to Kleisthenes' original ten must also have had repercussions on the political organization: the *Boule* was increased from 500 to 600 members, and certain colleges of magistrates (the *sitonai*, the *sophronistai*, etc.) were enlarged from ten to twelve members; but, in so far as most magistrates, even in Aristotle's day, had been appointed by all the demes together and not by individual tribes, the total number remained unaltered. Moreover, inscriptions prove the tendentious character of some of Plutarch's assertions; for instance, we have no proof of the replacement of the eponymous archon by the priest of the 'Saviour Gods'.[6]

In the purely administrative field, the progress achieved under Demetrios of Phaleron remained unaffected: for instance, the assumption by the state of responsibility for certain public expenses, which explains the increased importance of the official in charge of financial administration and of the various colleges of treasurers. But while the institutions themselves were little changed, the political climate was different from what it had been at the time of Demetrios of Phaleron.

Immediately after the entry of Demetrios Poliorketes into Athens, proceedings were instituted against those who had been close to his predecessor, the philosopher. Many of them fled without waiting for the people's verdict. Those who were actually brought to judgment were mostly acquitted. There was some destruction of the statues that had been raised to Demetrios, but contrary to what might have been expected the unrest seems to have died down very quickly.

Political conflicts, however, were by no means abandoned. It is possible to distinguish two main trends. The leading spirit of one of these was Stratokles. Plutarch portrays him as a base flatterer who showed his servility towards Demetrios and his father by proposing the title of *theoroi* for the ambassadors sent by the city to the two Kings, and instituting a veritable cult in their honour. According to Plutarch, Stratokles 'lived an abandoned life, and was thought to imitate the scurrility and buffoonery of the ancient Kleon in his familiarities with the people' (*Life of Demetrios*, 11).

Like Kleon, moreover, Stratokles appears to have been the butt of comedy, and the poet Philippides accuses him of being the cause of the sinister prodigies which Plutarch retails with a certain relish, and through which the gods were held to display their resentment at having a mere mortal preferred before them. We may wonder, however, if such a judgment should not be qualified. Stratokles was undoubtedly a demagogue, but the Hymn to Demetrios, although composed a few years later, proves that when he sought to confer divine honours on the two Kings he was expressing the will of the people. Moreover, in the troubled situation then prevailing in the Greek world, he knew that he could count on Demetrios and Antigonos to help Athens both to subsist and to face the hostility of Kassander. The dispatch of a consignment of wheat to cope with the food shortage and of cargoes of wood to enable the city-state to equip a fleet were not factors to be ignored. We must not forget that it was this same Stratokles who, shortly after the restoration of democracy, promoted a decree in honour of Lykourgos, the text of which has been preserved on two marble fragments (*I G* II² 457 = *Syll.*³ 326) and also by the author of the *Life of Lykourgos*. Now the text of the decree is highly revealing of the opinions professed by the Athenian politician: he praises Lykourgos for having contributed to the material restoration of the city and, moreover, for having retained his integrity and preserved the independence of the *polis* when under pressure from Alexander. Stratokles' aim must have been independence from Macedon and an effort towards internal recovery, and the evidence of his flattery of Demetrios should not blind us to this.

It is quite clear, however, that others, less perspicacious, were ready to outdo him in servility towards the master of the hour; for instance, that orator who, according to Plutarch, proposed that

> whenever Demetrios visited the city he should be received with the hospitable honours paid to Demeter and Dionysos, and that to the citizen who surpassed all others in the splendour and costliness of his reception, a sum of money should be granted from the public treasury for a dedicatory offering (*Life of Demetrios*, 12).

We may also assume that the decree proposed by one Sophokles of Sunion, forbidding the creation of new schools of philosophy in Athens without the authorization of the people, emanated from the same group of men, seeking in this way to forearm themselves against the ambitions of pupils of the Academy or the Lyceum. This decree, in any case, was rejected, and a suit brought against its author. Not long afterwards, in 306, Epicurus settled in Athens and founded his 'Garden' School, followed soon after by the Phoenician Zeno, the founder of Stoicism.

Are we to associate Demosthenes' nephew, the historian Demochares of Leukonoe, with this 'democratic' trend? He was to part company with Stratokles a few years later, and his growing antagonism towards Demetrios was to drive him into exile.[7] But in 307/6 he was probably still very close to the Stratokles set. A line of firm resistance to Kassander, then master of Macedonia, combined with an effort to restore Athens, could not fail to appeal to the man whom Polybios describes as a fierce opponent of Antipater and his successors (XII, 13). Unlike Stratokles or his own illustrious kinsman, Demochares was no orator. It was in his capacity as *strategos* that he promoted the repairing of the walls and fortifications of Athens,[8] as well as a diplomatic policy aimed at making Athens the centre of an alliance between Kassander's adversaries, and in particular at winning the friendship of the Boiotians.

Besides this democratic group, we may assume the existence of a group of 'moderates' who had accepted the authority of Demetrios of Phaleron and who, while rejoicing in the recovery of independence, could not but feel anxiety at the demagogic excesses to which the rule of Antigonos' son had given rise. One of the leaders of this moderate group was undoubtedly Phaidros of Sphettos, a rich man who owed part of his wealth to the mines and who, after the battle of Ipsos, was to play an important part in politics. The group also probably included Midias, the son of Demosthenes' wealthy opponent, the poet Philippides and others whom we do not know. These men, who represented the rich Athenian 'bourgeoisie', prized their city's independence, no doubt; but they must have felt that it was dearly paid for, since the alliance with Demetrios meant war against Kassander and consequently heavy financial burdens.

War had begun again, in fact, against Kassander on Greek soil, and Athens could count on only indirect assistance from Demetrios and his father, who were engaged in fighting against Ptolemy. During the first two years the war went well for the Athenians, and Kassander had to withdraw beyond Thermopylai. There were profuse expressions of gratitude towards Antigonos and Demetrios, who had sent respectively 150 talents and 1,200 pieces of armour taken at Salamis in Cyprus; meanwhile Demetrios' wife Phile was given divine honours and identified with Aphrodite.

At the beginning of 304 the situation suddenly deteriorated. Kassander succeeded in taking Salamis. Panic reigned in Athens. The *strategos* of the islands, Aeschetades, was held responsible for the defeat and sentenced accordingly, and an appeal was made to Demetrios. Having reorganized his fleet after its defeat in Egypt, Demetrios landed in Boiotia and forced Kassander to withdraw. Then he made a triumphal entry into Athens, welcomed once again as saviour by the Athenians. Plutarch writes:

> Although before they had used up and exhausted all the honours that could be bestowed upon him, [they] nevertheless devised a way to show themselves then also the authors of new and fresh flatteries. For instance, they assigned him the rear chamber of the Parthenon for his quarters; and there he lived, and there it was said that Athena received and entertained him (*Life of Demetrios*, 23).

It was at this time, during the winter of 304/3, that Demetrios, while living in Athens with the courtesan Lamia, indulged in those debaucheries which Plutarch, whatever he may say, relates with a certain relish.

The effect of Demetrios' presence in Athens was to sharpen the antagonism between his partisans and those who dreaded the consequences of his demagogic policy. The prosecution of Aeschetades recalled the dark days of Arginusai. The 'moderates' now took the offensive. Midias put to the Assembly's vote a decree in honour of Phokion. It was adopted, but soon afterwards attacked by Glaukippos, son of Hypereides. He failed to win a majority of votes, and the ashes of the old *strategos*, the friend of Antipater, were brought back to Athens.

Soon afterwards another incident was to intensify antagonisms still further. A certain Kleomedon, known to be a friend of Demetrios, was sentenced to a fine of fifty talents. The King, intervening for the first time in the affairs of the *polis*, had the verdict quashed. This appears to have caused some sensation. A decree was adopted by the Assembly, stipulating that the King should no longer be allowed to intervene in favour of any citizen by means of an official letter, as had happened in the case of Kleomedon. But shortly afterwards, under pressure from Demetrios, who 'was beyond measure incensed thereat, they took fright again, and not only rescinded the decree, but actually put to death some of those who had introduced and spoken in favour of it, and drove others into exile.' Moreover, they actually decreed, on the suggestion of Stratokles, that 'it was the pleasure of the Athenian people that whatsoever King Demetrios should ordain in future, this should be held righteous towards the gods and just towards men' (Plutarch, *Life of Demetrios*, 24). According to Plutarch, it was this affair that caused the rupture between Stratokles and Demochares, which was to result in the banishment of the latter.

Demetrios Poliorketes, meanwhile, despite the attractions of Lamia and his other courtesans, had not forgotten the tasks he had set himself and the demands of his struggle against Kassander. Already in 302, after his victorious campaign in the Peloponnese, he had summoned the delegates of the Greek states to a meeting on the Isthmus of Corinth and had renewed the Corinthian League with them.[9] Shortly after the condemnation of Demochares, he left Athens and went into Thessaly to resume the war against Kassander as leader of the Hellenic allies. But he was soon recalled to Asia by his father; and there, in the summer of 301, their army was defeated at Ipsos in Phrygia. Antigonos lost his life in this battle, while Demetrios became a fugitive, despite the secure position he still retained in the Aegean.

In Athens the news of the Ipsos disaster completed the discrediting of the friends of Poliorketes and of all those who, like Stratokles, had hoped to make use of that ruler's power to strengthen Athenian democracy. The moderate faction, led by such men as Phaidros of Sphettos, now came to the fore.[10] They did not, however, make a complete break with Demetrios yet, merely sending back his ships and his new wife, Deidarnia, whom he had left in Athens. In other respects a policy of neutrality and peace was pursued, and military expenses were drastically cut: from now on, military service ceased to be compulsory, and the period of training for *epheboi*, who were mainly recruited from well-to-do young Athenians, was reduced to one year. There was no question of reviving the system of restricted franchise, indeed, and it is significant that Demetrios of Phaleron was not asked to return to Athens; but neither was there any suggestion of reverting to the policy of restoring Athenian independence, for which Demochares and Stratokles had worked together before their quarrel, and although Stratokles suffered as a result of

Poliorketes' defeat, this did not mean that Demochares was recalled from exile. There may also have been certain constitutional changes at that time, in particular the appointment of magistrates by election instead of by lot. By the end of the fourth century, Athenian democracy seems to have become a mere formal relic, without substance. Even if there were some stirrings among the *demos* from time to time, on the occasion of some crisis or other, all real political power lay in the hands of a wealthy minority.

Athenian society at the end of the fourth century

Athenian society had undergone considerable changes since the beginning of the fourth century, when, despite the effects of the Peloponnesian war, it was still essentially rural, as we see from the later comedies of Aristophanes. The old civic community had consisted mainly of small and relatively well-off peasants and old aristocratic families, industry being in the hands of outsiders of recent citizenship or of dubious origin. It had now been replaced by a more highly differentiated society, within which economic interests had created fresh divisions. The legal speeches of the second half of the century, particularly those which form part of the Demosthenean *corpus*, the fragments of the Middle Comedy, and above all of the New Comedy, which have come down to us, and the *Characters* of Theophrastos enable us to sketch a picture of Athenian society during the last years of the fourth and the beginning of the third centuries, in which some blanks still remain but which none the less bears witness to the profound changes which had taken place during the century.[11]

We notice, in the first place, that the small peasant class had ceased to form the basis of Athenian democracy. This is clearly shown by the legal speeches, which deal essentially with the problems of townsfolk, and also by the plays of the time, particularly those of Menander. The peasants he depicts in the *Heautontimoroumenos*, in the *Dyskolos*, and in the *Georgos*, are rich peasants or well-to-do landowners, such as the father of Sostratos, in the *Dyskolos*, who is 'very wealthy, cultivates land worth many talents in the country, but lives in the city' (l. 39 ff.). The hero of the play, on the contrary, 'lives alone with his daughter and an old servant, carting wood, digging, toiling ceaselessly' (l. 327 ff.). But his son-in-law Gorgias repeatedly mentions that his land is worth at least two talents. Now when we consider that Antipater's decree, which fixed the sum required for full citizenship at 2,000 drachmas, excluded almost two-thirds of the Athenians from the citizen body, we see that Knemon is not really a poor man and that it is his character alone that explains the absence of servants from his home. On the other hand, the poor are often forced to hire themselves out for wages, or work to wipe out a debt. Thus in the *Hero* the children of Tibios work to pay back their father's debt to the rich master of Daos. Similarly Gorgias, in the play of that name, works on the land of the rich peasant Klainetos, while his mother and sister live in poverty in the town. The only poor peasant portrayed in Menander's plays is Gorgias in the *Dyskolos* (l. 23 ff.). He, however, is a victim of the ill-nature and avarice of Knemon, and, moreover, his marriage to the rich sister of Sostratos at the close of the play clearly betokens the end of his purely temporary misfortunes.

We thus witness the beginning of an evolution which was to grow more marked in the next century. On the one hand a well-to-do, indeed almost wealthy, peasantry, employing slave- or wage-labour to an increasing degree, and on the other the mass of poor people from whom these wage-labourers were drawn, or who left the country for the town or went even further afield. We know little about these poor people except that repeated efforts were made to deprive them of citizenship, and they must obviously have made up those chaotic and stormy Assemblies which played a part on several occasions towards the end of the century, in 318 at the trial of Phokion and in 307 when Demetrios Poliorketes entered Athens.

As for the rich, they certainly constituted a group which, to begin with, was far from homogeneous, but in which the gulf between town and country dwellers, so considerable at the beginning of the century, tended to decrease. We have already seen that Sostratos' father, while owning land to the value of several talents, lived in town and probably left the care of his estate to a steward. This must have been the case with many landowners whose property was on this scale. Those who, like Klainetos or Phainippos, lived on their estates were presumably anxious to make a profit from the produce of their lands. The rise in the price of agricultural products during the last decades of the fourth century, and the increasing difficulties of supply, tended to make agriculture a profitable activity, and this was unquestionably a new phenomenon.

But what we gather not only from the legal speeches of the late fourth century but also from the *Characters* of Theophrastos and the comedies of Menander is that these rich landowners did not object to increasing their wealth by advancing money in bottomry loans, and that ever closer links were thus formed between the old Athenian families and the business world.

The latter still consisted mainly, at the end of the fourth century, of foreigners, Greeks or barbarians, to whom collective or individual privileges were now granted on an ever-increasing scale, in particular the *enktesis ges kai oikias*, which was aimed at inducing them to settle in Athens. Athenian trade did in fact enjoy a revival of prosperity during the last decades of the fourth century. The vogue for the vases giving an effect of relief, in imitation of metal vases, of which Athens was, together with Southern Italy, the chief producer, explains this development and bears witness to its scale and importance.[12] A number of such vases have been found in Southern Russia, the region of the Bosphoros being still the chief source of Athens' corn supply, but also at the beginning of the third century in the new cities created by Alexander and his successors in Asia, Syria, Palestine and Egypt. It is therefore not surprising that rich citizens took an interest in these trading activities, either indirectly, through bottomry loans, or directly. Theophrastos' 'vain man' boasts of the considerable sums he has acquired through maritime trade (23, 4). In the following century, when Delos had become one of the pivots of Aegean trade, many Athenians were involved in the commercial activities of the island.[13]

Wealthy Athenians also held mining concessions. True, at the end of the fourth century we seem to be witnessing a decline in mining activity. The stocks of currency introduced into the Aegean market by Alexander's conquests dealt a serious blow to the preponderance of Athenian money; but before long, in the second half of the third century, the new Athenian coinage became widely used in the Aegean, and this again bears witness to the commercial influence of Athens. Although we lack documentary evidence on this point, we may assume that the mining industry enjoyed a revival of activity.

All this, needless to say, benefited chiefly a minority. It would be interesting to identify this minority more precisely. We are obviously obliged to make do with the names provided by inscriptions and literary texts. And here we are struck by the increasing scarcity of names belonging to the old families of Attica, which were still relatively numerous in the first half of the fourth century. The process was to be speeded up during the third century and still more in the second, when the increasingly generous granting of citizenship brought foreigners into the civic community. This new bourgeoisie, which did not disdain the profit to be got from exploiting land or from bottomry loans, which provided its daughters with rich dowries,[14] loved luxury and comfort and was prepared to give up any real independence for their sake.

The government of Demetrios of Phaleron was only a brief interval of 'philosophic' austerity. The restoration of democracy enabled the rich to revert to their habits of luxury, all the more shocking in contrast with the ever-growing distress of the poor. In the *Epitrepontes*, Charisios consoles himself for his wife's supposed infidelity by hiring a girl flute-player for twelve drachmas a day, 'enough for a man to live on for a month and six days'. Obviously the girl got only a tiny fraction of that sum, the profits going to her employer, the go-between who becomes a stock figure in comedy.

In fact, and this is the new factor which must be emphasized, for it is highly revealing, the growing importance of the love interest in the New Comedy is to be explained less by a change in sexual mores or the emancipation of women[15] than by the withdrawal of the bourgeois class from any real political activity. Whereas in the days of Aristophanes the problems of war and peace and the excesses of democracy were at the core of comic drama and often provided its plots (*Peace*, *Acharnians*, *Lysistrata*, *Ekklesiazusae*), in the New Comedy, although we occasionally find political allusions, they play no part in the development of the plot, which is essentially a love story. Theophrastos' *Characters* provide a gallery of portraits which only very exceptionally have a precise political context (friendly relations with Antipater, or the defence of oligarchy), which made it easy for La Bruyère to adapt them in the seventeenth century. This is no chance phenomenon, but reflects the Athenian bourgeoisie's growing detachment from political affairs, which were increasingly left to professional politicians, who tended to become administrators in a society where the *polis* had lost the power to make important decisions.

A brief account should be given of the other categories of the population, the resident foreigners and the slaves. The former, as we have seen, were still numerous at the end of the fourth century. The census made by Demetrios of Phaleron, in so far as it can be trusted, suggests that their number was about half that of the citizens, which is not inconsiderable. The development of economic life and the scale of commercial activities, of which the Piraeus was still the centre, readily explain the presence of many foreigners in Attica. Furthermore, and here we are reminded of the many suggestions made by Xenophon in *Ways and Means*, honours and privileges were granted to them by the *polis* on an ever increasing scale: decrees in favour of those who helped to ensure the city's supplies, tolerance towards the development of foreign forms of worship, the granting of *isoteleia* and *enktesis*.[16] It is not surprising, under these circumstances, that a large number of foreigners came to Athens and that some of them chose to reside there, at least for the time being. If we add to this the renown of Athenian schools of philosophy, we can account for the presence of a large foreign element in Athens. One final observation: the troubled period through which the city-state had passed during the closing years of the century must have enabled some of these aliens to penetrate into the civic body in a somewhat fraudulent fashion, since each reintroduction of democracy allowed them to evade the legal actions which would undoubtedly have been brought against them a few years earlier.

As for the slaves, they were certainly still very numerous on country estates as well as in the mines, factories and docks. There has been much questioning of the huge figure provided by Ktesikles.[17] It is unlikely, in fact, that Attica could have supported so large a slave population. It remains true, none the less, that slave-labour continued to be a feature of Athenian life. Slaves abound in Menander's comedies, and even poor peasants such as Gorgias have at least one. The growth of luxury promoted domesticity in Athenian homes, and the cook became a stock character in comedy. Needless to say, we must be content with very vague estimates, and we can neither give figures nor assess the exact role of slaves in production. But there does not seem to have been any notable change since the beginning of the century. If the price of slaves seems to have risen (5 to 7 *minai* against 2 or 3 when Xenophon wrote *Ways and Means*), this was a general phenomenon which does not imply a shortage. As to whether their condition had improved by the end of the century, this is a relatively secondary problem. As we learn from the vases (*phiales*) dedicated by freedmen to the tutelary goddess of Athens, manumission was only granted to a small number of slaves, and then always on an individual basis.[18] Although the slave who is his master's confidant, or the faithful old nurse, remain stock figures of the New Comedy, this does not imply any general improvement in the lot of slaves. The revolt of the Laurion miners at the end of the second century gives evidence that for them things had scarcely changed since the time of Dekeleia.

We should like to be able to say more; but our sources are too fragmentary, too incomplete to allow of any definitive conclusions. One thing remains certain: Athenian society at the end of the fourth century was no longer that isonomic community of citizen-soldiers, attached to their own small domain and prepared to do anything to defend it. The love of money and luxury had become powerful factors in transforming a society which, with a few exceptions, had lost all ambition for great deeds. True, in some particular context that ambition might revive, out of family tradition in some cases, out of despair in others; but it no longer constituted the very foundation of the *polis*. Some citizens sought primarily to enrich themselves through trade, through speculation, through military or civilian service in the pay of a foreign ruler—although relatively few Athenians left their native land—and the rest sought to subsist by battling with 'rocks that bore nothing but thyme and sage' (*Dyskolos*, l. 604).

6 The final upsurge of nationalism: the Chremonidean war. Athens loses her independence and her political importance

At the onset of the third century, the issues were not yet clearly decided in the Eastern basis of the Mediterranean. It was to be almost a quarter of a century more before the general structure of the Hellenistic world took shape, in particular before the Antigonids seized control of Macedonia. This was obviously the essential problem as far as the Greek city-states were concerned, since the personality of the Macedonian ruler would determine their greater or less degree of independence. And it was during the first quarter of the third century that they began to look towards Egypt for possible, if remote, support. When in 276 Gonatas became the unquestioned master of Macedonia, it was with the help of Egypt that the Greeks prepared the last great 'national' uprising in their history.

The new conditions of political life in Athens at the beginning of the third century

We have already seen the effects on Athenian life of the defeat at Ipsos. All those who found it hard to tolerate the sway of Demetrios, and especially his open support of the orators of the people's party, had recovered hope. Under moderate leaders such as Phaidros of Sphettos, certain constitutional measures had provided the democratic regime with a content more in keeping with new social realities; but these measures had obviously not gone unchallenged. It is in this context that we must consider the 'tyranny' of Lachares.[1] Ferguson thinks that Lachares must have been one of Phaidros' group of friends. He may also have already been in contact with

Kassander. However, a fragment of papyrus, studied by de Sanctis, prompts one to qualify Ferguson's assertions. It seems, in fact, that in 297/6 Lachares was *strategos* of the foreigners, and that it was with the support of the Piraeus garrison that he took power as a tyrant. Or, more precisely, it was with the support of the Piraeus garrison that he succeeded in expelling the *strategos* of the hoplites, Charis, from the town and from the Acropolis. Taken in conjunction with these data, discovered by de Sanctis, a certain passage from Pausanias sheds light on the events which took place in Athens in 197/6. He tells us: 'Kassander, inspired by a fierce hatred of the Athenians, won the friendship of Lachares, who hitherto had been the leader of the people's party (*proestekota es ekeino tou demou*), and incited him to establish a tyranny' (I, xxv, 7). According to this version, Lachares had belonged to the people's party and it was under cover of the disturbances due to the shortage of wheat and the anti-democratic measures taken by the moderate group to which Charis, *strategos* of the hoplites, presumably belonged, that he seized power as tyrant, with the backing of the Piraeus, the traditional stronghold of democracy in Athens. But as a personal friend of Kassander, Lachares quickly came to represent to Athenian eyes the power of Macedon. Hence the growing hostility of the Piraeus garrison, and the appeal to Demetrios by those who saw Lachares as Kassander's man. Hence, too, the traditional hostility towards Lachares which Pausanias echoes when he writes: 'We know of no other tyrant so cruel towards men and so impious towards the gods' (ibid.).

Demetrios lost no time in responding to the appeal of his supporters; he seized Eleusis and Rhamnonte, and began to lay siege to Athens. Lachares then tightened up his tyranny. He appointed a new *Boule* and new magistrates, and resorted to various extortionate measures to ensure the payment of his soldiers (Pausanias I, xxix, 16). At the same time a decree was issued against the accomplices of Demetrios, and contacts were established with Ptolemy.

The situation in Athens grew steadily worse. Kassander, from whom Lachares might have expected help, was dead, and Egyptian aid was uncertain, to say the least. In the city, the price of barley and wheat rose constantly, owing to the increasing difficulties of supply; wheat even reached the incredible price of 300 drachmas the *medimnos*. Demetrios seems to have been partly responsible for these difficulties. According to Plutarch, he was laying waste the Athenian

countryside around Rhamnonte and Eleusis. Furthermore, he inter-
cepted a ship carrying wheat and had the merchant and the pilot
hanged, the result of which was to deter trading ships from visiting
Athens.

It is thus not surprising that after the departure of the fleet sent by
Ptolemy, which had not joined battle with Demetrios, the Athenians
drove out Lachares and opened their gates to Demetrios Poliorketes.
The tyrant fled into Boiotia, 'taking with him the gold bucklers from
the Acropolis and the ornaments of Athene's statue' (Pausanias I,
25). He was later murdered by the people of Koronea.

Plutarch's account gives us a glimpse of the situation prevailing in
Athens in the summer of 294:

> Then the Athenians, although they had decreed death for anyone
> who should so much as mention peace and reconciliation with
> Demetrios, straightway threw open the nearest gates and sent
> ambassadors to him. They did not expect any kindly treatment
> from him, but were driven to the step by their destitution, in which,
> among other grievous things, the following also is said to have
> occurred. A father and a son were sitting in a room and had aban-
> doned all hope. Then a dead mouse fell from the ceiling, and the
> two, when they saw it, sprang up and fought with one another for it.
> At this time also, we are told, the philosopher Epicurus sustained the
> lives of his associates with beans, which he counted out and distri-
> buted among them. Such, then, was the plight of the citizens when
> Demetrios made his entry, and ordered all the people to assemble in
> the theatre. He fenced the stage-buildings round with armed men,
> and encompassed the stage itself with his body-guards, while he
> himself, like the tragic actors, came down into view through one of
> the upper side-entrances. The Athenians were more than ever
> frightened now; but with the first words that he uttered Demetrios
> put an end to their fears. For avoiding all harshness of tone and
> bitterness of speech, he merely chided them lightly and in a friendly
> manner, and then declared himself reconciled, gave them besides a
> hundred thousand bushels of grain, and established the magistrates
> who were most acceptable to the people. So Dromokleides the
> orator, seeing that the people, in their joy, were shouting all sorts of
> proposals, and were eager to outdo the customary eulogies of the
> public speakers on the *bema* [rostrum], brought in a motion that
> Piraeus and Munychia should be handed over to Demetrios the

King. This was voted, and Demetrios on his own account put a garrison in the Museum also, that the people might not again shake off the yoke and give him further trouble (*Life of Demetrios*, 34).[2]

This text is interesting in that it shows how far the situation in Athens had deteriorated. In order to survive, its leaders were prepared to descend to every kind of servility towards Demetrios and even to accept the loss of that which, for some of them, had formerly justified their alliance with him, namely independence guaranteed by the removal of the Macedonian garrison from Munychia. Now, the presence of a garrison in the Museum meant that it was not only the Piraeus which was being kept under surveillance, but the city itself. Against this the people assembled in the theatre could do nothing, and even if some of their democratic institutions were restored, this obviously meant very little. It is hard to say, moreover, precisely what this restoration consisted of: perhaps merely of a return to the collegiate principle for certain magistracies, such as that of superintendent of the financial administration. This, however, was a pure formality.

The proof, moreover, that the 'restoration' of democracy by Demetrios had no real political significance is that the principal magistrates' posts were occupied by men who had withdrawn from the scene after 302, such as Stratokles, as well as by moderate leaders such as Phaidros or Philippides.

Meanwhile, however, the evolution of the general situation was to have its repercussions on Athenian political life. In the autumn of that same year, 294, Demetrios, having settled matters in Athens, moved into Macedonia, and having got rid of the two sons of Kassander, who had succeeded their father, had himself proclaimed King of Macedon by his army. He was to hold this title until 288, when, driven out by Lysimachos and Pyrrhos, he fled into Asia where, two years later, he fell into the hands of Seleukos. Having become master of Macedonia, Poliorketes, that former champion of Greek liberty against Kassander, was to adopt on his own account the policy of his old adversary, a policy based on securing the submission of the Greek city-states. In Athens, which he used as his capital, he met with increasing opposition, and while some hopes were turned once again towards Egypt, whither Phaidros of Sphettos went on an embassy in 292, Demetrios' decree, ordering the return of those banished, aroused violent resentment. The chronology of events is not easy to establish; but there seems to have been some unrest in Athens while Demetrios was at Corcyra. This had little effect, however. It was on the occasion of Demetrios' return from his expedition to the West that the hymn in his honour was composed; it reflects the servility of his worshippers, but also the distress of the Athenian people. Athens remained, moreover, the focus of Demetrios' power. He held the Pythian games there when they could not be celebrated at Delphi as was customary, owing to the threat to the sanctuary from the Aitolians; and this justifies Plutarch's comment that 'he was more solicitous for the favour of the Athenians than for that of any other Greeks' (*Life of Demetrios*, 42). And the fleet that he proposed sending to Asia was built, in part at least, in Athens.

Nevertheless, his position in Greece itself was increasingly precarious. Threatened in the West by Pyrrhos, in the East by Lysimachos and Seleukos, and in the islands by Ptolemy, he saw his authority declining. Those Athenians who were becoming increasingly restive under his sway entered into negotiations with his main adversary, Lysimachos, who had given shelter in Thrace to the exiled Demochares. A decree brought the historian home, while the Athenians took advantage of Demetrios' difficulties to expel the garrison from the Museum and recover Eleusis. At the same time the opponents of Poliorketes contributed financially to Athens' recovery, her wheat supply being secured by a consignment of 15,000 *medimnai* from Spartakos, King of Bosphoros. When Demetrios came to besiege Athens he met with fierce resistance, and being threatened by Pyrrhos, he decided to raise the siege. None the less he was still master of the Piraeus, of the forts of Panakton and Phyle, and of the cleruchy islands. An attempt to recapture the Piraeus failed, and 419 Athenians died in the operation. Their sacrifice was commemorated by a monument erected in the Kerameikon, which Pausanias saw during his travels (I, xxix, 10). At the same time a new embassy, led by Philippides, was sent to Lysimachos.

The adventurous life of Demetrios Poliorketes was nearing its end. In 288, he was forced to flee from his kingdom, which had been seized by Lysimachos and Pyrrhos; in 286 he was taken prisoner by Seleukos, and he died three years later without recovering his liberty.[3]

He had left his son Antigonos in Greece. Did Antigonos succeed in maintaining his position in the Piraeus? The question is still being debated. Ferguson concludes affirmatively, on the grounds that the chief of the Macedonian garrison was the same man, Hierokles the Carian, before 286 and after 276; but other modern scholars suggest dates for the expulsion of the garrison which vary between 280 and 272.[4] In fact, apart from an attack on Eleusis by Antigonos, which was successfully repulsed by Olympiodoros, there was no real threat to Athens during the ensuing years. It was in Asia that everything was really being decided at this vital moment. Even if we admit that the Macedonian garrison remained in control of the Piraeus, the position of Athens seems to have been relatively favourable; in 280 at the latest, Antiochos I, who had succeeded his father Seleukos, re-stored to the Athenians the cleruchy islands which Seleukos had recovered from Demetrios. The Athenians might well be under the illusion that they had regained their former independence, and the erection of a statue in honour of Demosthenes in 280/79 shows that they now considered themselves free from Macedonian control.

The renewal of the struggle against Macedon: the Chremonidean war

The anarchy that prevailed in Macedonia obviously helped to foster that illusion, as did the relative stability now achieved in the East; but the Celtic invasion was to provide Antigonos Gonatas, hitherto a 'king without a kingdom',[5] with the opportunity to become master of Macedonia. The victory he won at Lysimacheia secured for him the kingdom which his father had been forced to abandon eleven years previously.

The re-establishment of a single authority in Macedon, and the personality of the new King, were to decide the evolution of the situation in Athens. The son of Poliorketes had in fact spent part of his youth there. He had, in particular, been a pupil of Zeno in the Stoa, and he maintained friendly relations all his life with many of his former fellow-students. He himself often stayed in Athens after he had become King of Macedonia. His son by the courtesan Demo was brought up in an atmosphere of Stoicism, and his two half-brothers, Krateros and Demetrios, also lived in Athens; but it was not merely from personal feelings that Gonatas remained faithful to

Athens. He wanted to put into practice the teaching of his master, Zeno, he intended to be a philosopher-king, considered his duty as a noble bondage, and sought to realize in his political actions the doctrines he had learned in Athens.[6] He was therefore anxious to reach agreement with the Greeks, as his father Demetrios had done, all the more since his authority in Macedonia was now secure; but on condition of preserving certain vital positions by maintaining garrisons at the main strategic points.[7]

In Athens there was no lack of support for a policy of alliance with Gonatas. This was upheld by all those who, for fear of a revival of political and social unrest, remained faithful to the pro-Macedonian party, particularly as the power of Macedon was now embodied in a a man who was known to have links with Athens. Antigonos had given the Athenians back the forts which had remained under his control after his father's death. As we have seen earlier, the Macedonian garrison may possibly have been withdrawn from the Piraeus for a few years. Men of the moderate party, such as Phaidros of Sphettos, could therefore associate themselves with the traditional pro-Macedonians in order to achieve a *rapprochement* with Gonatas. A decree (*I G* II² 683) records the people's vote for a sacrifice for the prosperity of the Athenians and of King Gonatas. At the great Panathenaia of 274, paintings commemorating the victory of Gonatas over the Celts were dedicated in the sanctuary of Athene Nike by a certain Herakleitos (*I G* II² 677 = *Syll.*³ 401).

However, if the great majority of influential political men were in favour of a policy of friendly neutrality towards Antigonos, there remained none the less a small nucleus whose opposition was unshakable. What did they represent? The *demos* as opposed to the pro-Macedonian oligarchs? As in the days of Demosthenes and Philip, the answer is not so simple. True, there no doubt existed a group of men who clung doggedly to the political attitudes of the preceding century, even though they put up with the new state of affairs. Thus when Demochares died, his son Laches had a decree passed in his honour (pseudo-Plutarch, *Life of the Ten Orators*, 151) in which no reference was made to the presence of the Macedonian, or to the connection which might have existed between that presence and the exile of Demochares, which was represented as a manoeuvre by the 'oligarchs'. The same refusal to face the new situation with regard to Macedon recurs in the decree proposed by Chremonides, during the archonship of Pitidemos, which was to result in war

(*I G* II² 686–687 = *Syll.*³ 434/5).⁸ This decree referred to the former alliance between Sparta and Athens for the defence of freedom against the barbarian, and criticized those men in the city-states who were prepared to destroy the *patrios politeia*.⁹ Here were mingled all the elements of the democratic tradition, an appeal to a bygone past of which, from family loyalty, a small group of men still dreamed, the most notable of them, since the death of Demochares, being the two sons of Eteokles of the deme of Aithalidai, Glaukon and Chremonides.

Chremonides, however, does not seem to have played a decisive political role before the outbreak of the war which was already known by his name in ancient times.¹⁰ Whereas his brother had been a hierophant at Eleusis and is known through certain inscriptions (*I G* II² 1933 = *Syll.*³ 1022; *I G* II² 3845), while his sister Phidostrate had been priestess of Aglauros (*I G* II² 3459) and his elder brother Glaukon an Olympic winner (*Syll.*³ 462 1.3), Chremonides appears chiefly as a thinker, a disciple of Zeno, whose teaching he followed faithfully. It is the more surprising to find him at the head of a coalition (which indeed his name came to symbolize) the object of which was to deliver the Greece of the city-states from the domination of a man who had also been a pupil of the Stoic philosopher, and who had remained faithful to his teaching. In fact, as has been shown in a stimulating article by Franco Sartori,¹¹ the Stoic ideal played practically no part in determining the behaviour of Chremonides. Under the influence of a staunchly traditionalist family, the young man forgot the teaching of his master in an attempt to revive old-time values. The decree to which we have already referred might well have been drawn up a century earlier, for its themes—the struggle against the barbarian, the defence of Greek liberty—were part of the armoury of fourth-century political propaganda; while the allusion to the *patrios politeia* tells us clearly enough that Chremonides remembered the teaching of Isokrates (*Panegyric*, *Areopagiticus*) better than that of Zeno of Kition.

We should, however, misunderstand the Chremonidean war if we saw it merely as the last spasmodic effort of a political class. The Greek world was no longer free to make its own decisions, and it has long been recognized that the Ptolemaic sovereigns played an important part in this affair, notably the ambitious Arsinoe, wife and sister of Philadelphos.¹² This is not the place to recall the intrigues of that queen during the last years of her life, aimed at ensuring the possession of Macedon for the son she had had by Lysimachos. We may wonder, however, whether too much importance has not been ascribed to these intrigues, as also to the relations between Arsinoe and the groups of Athenian exiles in Alexandria. Similarly we should beware of over-stressing the economic causes of the Chremonidean war—Philadelphos was not trying to control the wheat market in the Aegean, at all events beyond his immediate possessions, and if the need to ensure the city's supplies explains the continuous contact between certain Athenian politicians and the Alexandrian court, this was a constant factor in Athenian policy to which we should not ascribe an overriding importance at this precise juncture.[13] As for the idea put forward by Rostovtzeff that Philadelphos, when he provoked the Chremonidean war, wanted to prevent Antigonos from making the Piraeus 'a rival, as it were, to Rhodes and Delos, the great *emporia* of the Ptolemies', it seems far too 'modernistic'. There is no need to seek out such complex reasons. In the struggle for hegemony in the Aegean sea, the Ptolemies were naturally tempted to rely on all those who, in the more or less submissive city-states of Greece, were anxious, whether out of loyalty to a bygone ideal or out of self-interest, to throw off the Macedonian yoke. Rome was to act in the same way in the following century.

The time indeed may have seemed ripe: the modern historian reckons that Gonatas' position was secure by then in Macedonia, but contemporaries may not have felt equally certain. The very moderation of Demetrios' son acted against him and aroused all sorts of hopes. In Greece itself, the influence of Macedon was then precarious, to say the least. Boiotians and Aitolians controlled central Greece. In the Peloponnese the king of Sparta, Areus, a man of powerful personality who had defeated Pyrrhos, sought to reconstitute Peloponnesian unity.[14] To the Ptolemies, the situation thus seemed favourable for an enterprise intended to nip in the bud Antigonos' pretensions to hegemony in the Aegean; and Athenian circles in Alexandria were well able to provide Ptolemaic propaganda with the ideological substratum most apt to win over the majority of Greek states, which finds its most complete expression in the decree of Chremonides.

The war broke out shortly after the Assembly's adoption of that decree, which bears the date of the archonship of Pitidemos (according to modern scholars, between 269/8 and 266/5).[15] From the beginning, the coalition revealed its weakness; Areus, king of Sparta, failed to take Corinth and met his death almost immediately. Athens had to face Macedon practically alone, and endured a two-year siege at the end of which she capitulated (263/2). The Ptolemaic navy had been no help at all, either because the support actually provided by Ptolemy was very slight or, which is more likely, because he was prevented from fulfilling his obligations by Gonatas' threat to the Asian coasts; Egyptian troops did indeed land in Attica, under the command of the Ptolemaic admiral Patrokles (cf. the discoveries at Koroni), but did not succeed in freeing the city.[16]

Gonatas meanwhile had had to face an attack by Alexander of Epiros. He succeeded none the less in getting the better of the allies, and the naval victory which he won over the Ptolemaic fleet off Kos strengthened his position still further.[17]

Now that he was master of Athens, he exercised direct control over the city-state for some years. Macedonian garrisons were established at Sounion, at Salamis, at Panakton, at Phyle, at Rhamnonte, and within the city itself, in the Museum. Hierokles was put at the head of all the Macedonian troops stationed in Attica. Furthermore, the men who had directed Athenian policy during the war were driven into exile and replaced by a new group, more subservient to Macedon. Finally, Athens lost, for a few years, the right to coin money. But there were, strictly speaking, no constitutional changes. One must be wary of tradition in this respect: we do not know exactly of what liberties Gonatas deprived the Athenians, restoring them a few years later, in 256/5; it has been shown, on the basis of epigraphic documents, that there were still some Macedonian garrisons in Attic forts after this date.[18] More probably, there may have been some relaxation of political control.

The diminishing importance of Athens

It is certain, at all events, that the victory of Antigonos meant the end of Athenian dreams of independence. The same period witnessed the death of those men who, born in the last third of the fourth century, had known an Athens that was still powerful and free, and who had never given up hope of seeing that Athens reborn.

Pre-eminent among these was the historian Philochoros, the last of the Atthidographers.[19] He was probably born about 340. He died soon after the capitulation of Athens, in circumstances which are not clear, either executed on the King's orders or condemned by a regular court. There is no doubt, in fact, that without being directly involved in political life he had belonged to the group of men who had prepared the Chremonidean war. He may have been equally responsible with the Alexandrian exiles for providing the anti-Macedonian party with its ideological substratum—the appeal to the past greatness of Athens and to the *patrios politeia*, to independence with regard to Macedon, and the safeguarding of Athenian liberty, his line being akin to that which Lykourgos had successfully put forward while Philocheros was still a boy. Once again, through the example of the last Athenian historian, we see how risky it is to equate the supporters of democracy with the opponents of Macedon. In this connection, the victory of Antigonos did not imply that the oligarchs had triumphed in Athens; and even if certain circles still clung to the identification of democracy with hostility to Macedon, formerly advanced by Demosthenes, it now bore no relation to reality. The Chremonidean war had been sought by men of moderate tendencies, friends of Demochares; and their defeat, more than the triumph of any particular party, meant that Athens was finally losing all importance as a political power.

Another thinker who died at about the same time was Zeno, founder of the Stoic school and teacher of Antigonos. Born at Kition in Cyprus, he had come to Athens in 311, and had studied first under the Cynic, Krates, and then under Polemon at the Academy. In 301 he founded his own school, the Stoa, which was to attract many young Athenians of good family and foreigners. Whereas the Academy and the Lyceum remained faithful to the teaching of their founders, who saw the *polis* as the ideal setting which alone could enable man to fulfil himself, the Stoic school, heir to the Cynics, proposed the wider setting of the whole *oikoumene*. Plutarch writes:

> The much admired *politeia* of Zeno, who founded the Stoic sect, has for its general aim that we should discontinue living in separate cities and peoples, differentiated by varying conceptions of justice, and instead regard all men as members of one city and one people, having one life and one order as a herd feeding together is reared on a common pasture.[20]

We can see why such an ideal appealed to the son of Poliorketes, and why he not only maintained good personal relations with the head and founder of the school, but also sought to attract to his court some of his fellow-pupils, including the famous Perseus, and attempted to solve the contradiction between his philosophic aspirations and the concrete reality of his authority by setting philosopher-tyrants over the city-states under his sway. His relatively moderate attitude towards the Athenians can be explained by the presence in Athens of his old master, and the honours he paid to Zeno after the philosopher's death bear witness to his loyalty and to his attachment.[21]

In point of fact, the problem, for which many solutions, often contradictory, have been offered ever since the appearance of W. S. Ferguson's book on Hellenistic Athens and that of W. W. Tarn on Gonatas, is to know how, and how far, Gonatas exercised his power as *tyrannos* over Athens after the defeat of Chremonides and his friends. One thing remains certain: even if the garrison was withdrawn from the Museum in 256/5, giving the Athenians a temporary sense of liberation, Gonatas' troops remained stationed in the forts of Attica. The fact that they were placed under the command of an Athenian adherent of Macedon, Herakleitos of Athmonon,[22] does not imply any relaxation of the close watch being kept on Athens. Apart from this, Gonatas, faithful in this respect to his father's policy as much as to that formerly laid down by Philip and Alexander, did not seek to control institutions directly, nor to alter the Athenian constitution. It was much simpler to make sure of having reliable men at the head of the principal magistracies. Furthermore, his military control of Athens provided Antigonos with a guarantee of its citizens' loyalty.

It is a striking fact, none the less, that until the death of the king the Athenians made no attempt to escape from a yoke which was presumably not very heavy, and which must have brought them privileges and material advantages. It is significant that when war revived between Antigonos and Ptolemy, Athens remained loyal to Antigonos despite the presence of Chremonides and Glaukon at the head of the Ptolemaic fleet. We can be sure that Philadelphos and, after him, Euergetes made numerous approaches to Athens in the hope of bringing her back into the camp of Gonatas' enemies. When these approaches failed they resorted to force; thus Aratos made repeated efforts to 'liberate' the Athenians from

Macedonian domination, but on each occasion met with resistance from the Athenians (cf. Plutarch, *Life of Aratos*, 33, 34).[23]

The death of Antigonos in 239 did not alter the situation. While his successor, Demetrios II, had to face a coalition of the two great Greek leagues, the Athenians remained neutral and repelled the fresh attacks directed against the Piraeus by the *strategos* of the Achaean League. However, these repeated incursions on to Athenian territory inevitably entailed serious damage. An effort was therefore made to repair the frontier forts, under the energetic leadership of Aristophanes of Leukonoe, *strategos* of the foreigners and later of Eleusis. To cover the expense required for territorial defence there was instituted an *epidosis*, a sort of loan from the richest of the Athenians, whose gifts and subscriptions made it possible to carry out the work and to ensure the food supplies of townsfolk and country folk. For Aratos' repeated inroads had wrought considerable havoc, and the situation was increasingly tense.

We cannot wonder, then, that at the death of Demetrios II, whose successor was a seven-year-old child, some Athenians envisaged throwing off the yoke of Macedon and making peace with Aratos and the Achaean League. This movement was initiated by Eurykleides of Kephisia, a rich and influential citizen, who had been treasurer of the military exchequer in 232/1 and had spent some seven talents the following year as *agonothetes* of the Panathenaia. Eurykleides belonged to that wealthy middle class which had accepted Macedonian domination when it meant the maintenance of peace and internal order, but was ready to reject it as soon as it involved Athens in excessive expenditure.

Things happened very peacefully, however. Eurykleides and his friends appealed to Aratos, who, being a sick man, was no longer *strategos* of the Achaean League but who still guided its policy.

> He was carried in a litter to help the city in its time of need, and joined in persuading Diogenes, the commander of the garrison, to give up the Piraeus, Munychia, Salamis and Sounion to the Athenians, for a hundred and fifty talents, twenty of which Aratos contributed himself (Plutarch, *Life of Aratos*, 34).

Once the city was free of its Macedonian garrison, however, those who had worked for its liberation were wary of being drawn into the opposite camp. Eurykleides and his brother Mikion,[24] who were then leading figures in Athenian political life and were to continue so for almost thirty years, refused to act in concert with Aratos (Plutarch, ibid. 41).

This marked the triumph of a policy of absolute neutrality, on which Polybios was to pass severe judgment:

> The Athenians were now delivered from the fear of Macedonia and regarded their liberty as securely established. Following the policy and inclinations of their leading statesmen Eurykleides and Mikion, they took no part in the affairs of the rest of Greece, but were profuse in their adulation of all the kings, and chiefly of Ptolemy, consenting to every variety of decree and proclamation, however humiliating, and paid little heed to decency in this respect owing to the lack of judgement of their leaders (V, 106).[25]

This extremely severe criticism by Polybios is to be explained by the fact that Athens had refused to join Aratos and the Achaean League. In point of fact, the long period which followed, during which Eurykleides and Mikion dominated Athenian political life, appears to have been one of relative prosperity, despite the undoubted dwindling of the city's importance.

The mines were put into working order again and a new Athenian coinage was issued, which quite soon circulated widely.[26] The departure of the Macedonian garrison from the Piraeus enabled the port to recover its former activity which, however, remained strictly limited. Whereas at the beginning of the century the export of Attic vases showed that the Piraeus was still the centre of commercial life, in the second half of the century trade shifted towards the East and in particular towards Rhodes. One proof of this decline of the Piraeus was the neglect of the Long Walls, which remained in ruins, while at the same period the fortifications of the town and the port were being repaired so as to form two separate defensive systems. The care taken in restoring the border fortresses, and the expense incurred through these reparations, at a time when Athens had only limited funds at her disposal, show clearly that the defence of her territory had now become of prime importance, and that she intended to guard against any recurrence of raids like those of Aratos. Another fact provides evidence: the legislative measures aimed at preventing immigrants, or Athenians recently admitted to citizenship, from acquiring land unrestrictedly, the *enktesis ges* being no longer granted without restriction but according to a maximum fixed by law, varying between a thousand drachmas for a house and two talents for a piece of land. The most ancient inscription recording the granting of restricted *enktesis* dates, in fact, from the first half of the third century (*I G* II² 706), and is thus prior to the period of Eurykleides and Mikion; but it is significant that this restriction recurs in all subsequent formulations of *enktesis*.[27] This tends to prove that

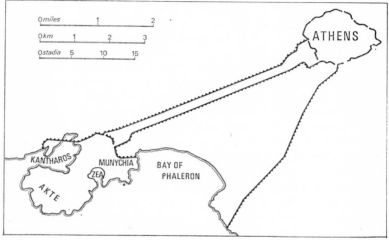

Athens, Piraeus and the Long Walls

foreigners residing in Athens, even if they had come there to trade, were trying to acquire landed property there, and that Athenian landowners wanted to protect themselves against such a seizure of the city's territory. We cannot help recalling the provisions set forth by Plato in the *Laws*, which dealt only with goods and chattels, the only form of property which foreigners were then allowed to own. True, we must beware of hasty conclusions, considering the scarcity of the inscriptions available, but we have here a valuable pointer none the less. This predominance of the landowning interests over the trading interests of the *polis* can be traced even in the new urban development. The second half of the third century was in fact a period of considerable building activity, particularly in the neighbourhood of the Agora, in the eastern and north-eastern districts, where the sanctuary of the Graces was erected (its priests provided by the family of Eurykleides) and also new gymnasia, including the

Ptolemaion. These buildings herald the great constructions which, in the following century, Athens owed to the generosity of the Attalids.[28]

Indeed, the architectural rebirth of the city was achieved less through its own resources or the wealth of the middle-class Athenians who governed the *polis* than through the generosity of the 'Kings'. Eurykleides and Mikion had won the favour of Doson, who soon appeared to all the Greeks as a bulwark of order against the revolutionary enterprises of the King of Sparta, Kleomenes, and the unrest developing in the Peloponnese.[29] Athens had already entered into relations with Attalos I of Pergamon, and these relations were to become closer in the following century; but in this second half of the third century it was Euergetes, above all, who appeared as the natural protector of the Athenians.[30] We have already noted the close links existing in the preceding period between Athens and Alexandria. These were maintained and strengthened during the second half of the century, all the more so because the power of Egypt seemed less directly threatening. Euergetes became the eponymous hero of a new tribe, while a cult was vowed to him and to his wife Berenike, and Ptolemaia were celebrated regularly. The creation of a thirteenth tribe inevitably posed constitutional problems. It is significant, as Ferguson notes,[31] that there was no suggestion of suppressing the two tribes created in honour of Antigonos and Demetrios. By including among their eponymous heroes the ancestors of the royal families of Macedon and Egypt the Athenians were indeed 'prostrating themselves before kings of all sorts'.

The relative prosperity of Athens was in sharp contrast with the extreme poverty of the Hellenic world. Towards 205 a traveller, Herakleides the Critic, gave a description which deserves to be quoted at length:[32]

> Thence to Athens. The road is pleasant, the land all cultivated, the prospect inviting. The city is everywhere dry, water being scarce; and because of its age, the streets and blocks are irregular. Most of the houses are mean, the nice ones few. A stranger would doubt, on seeing it first, if this were really the renowned city of the Athenians. After a little, however, he would be convinced. An Odeion, the finest in the world; a notable theatre, large and excellent; a costly temple of Athena, far-visible and well worth a visit, overhanging the theatre, the so-called Parthenon. It makes a great impression upon

the spectator. An Olympeion, half finished but displaying the general plan. It would be the best if it were completed. Three gymnasia—Academia, Lyceum, Kynosarges—with grounds thickly wooded and grassy, schools of philosophers of every shade of opinion. . . . Banquets of all sorts, many snares and recreations of the spirit, unceasing shows. . . . In a word, Athens surpasses other cities in all that makes for the enjoyment and betterment of life.

We should not delude ourselves, however. Even though Athens might still seem to a passing stranger a place of delights, satisfying both soul and body, her sometime greatness lay a long way back. The political regime which had brought her glory still stood, and the forms of democracy were respected; but in reality a small group of men, rich landowners, dominated political life, and the Assembly merely ratified decisions which it had no part in taking. Similarly, the army had ceased to be a citizen army, although there were many Athenians among the mercenaries stationed at Eleusis and in the various forts. The leaders of that army, while respecting political forms inherited from a remote past, had full powers to control them as they chose.

Finally, the schools of philosophy which, during the first half of the century, had brought Athens her renown, were declining too. After the death of the two great masters who had founded the Epicurean and Stoic schools, rifts had developed among their followers. A few great names had still dominated the mid-century, notably that of Kleanthes of Assos, who succeeded Zeno at the head of the Stoic school. The decline of these schools of philosophy is not surprising; the appeal of the great Eastern courts had proved irresistible to most men. Furthermore, that philosophy was intimately bound up with the civilization of the city which now lay dying. Politics, in Athens, had become increasingly the business of professionals, who managed public finance and made rules for the administration without feeling bound to refer to lofty principles. Athens had lost all hegemonic ambitions, and also the concept of a *polis* as the final aim for mankind. Only the Stoic cosmopolitanism which asserted itself at the end of the century with Chrysippos bore some relation to the new reality which had developed during the century.

By 203, when the two brothers died who had governed Athens for a quarter of a century, Athenian greatness was definitely a thing of the past; and in the last upsurge of Hellenism against the growing power of Rome, Athens had become no more than a humble pawn on a chessboard which now extended over the entire Mediterranean.

7   Athens and Rome

During the greater part of the third century, the problem that dominated the history of Athens was that of her relations with the two great monarchies which had endeavoured to control the Aegean, the Antigonid and the Ptolemaic; but the end of the century witnessed the appearance in Greece of the power of Rome, and from that time onward relations with Rome were to play a leading part in the history of the Greek world, more particularly in that of Athens, which for over a century was to be one of the props of Roman power on the Hellenic mainland.

Since the accession of Philip, Athens had observed the neutrality to which she had pledged herself in her agreement with Antigonos Doson. Thus, when during the crisis of 218 Megaleas sought refuge in Athens, the Athenians refused to shelter him.[1] Again, a few years later, when the first Macedonian war broke out, Athens remained neutral. The break with Philip was to be determined by an apparently trivial incident. Two young Akarnanians had, by fraud, taken part in the initiation ceremonies at Eleusis. They were put to death. Now Akarnania was under Philip's protection; he could not let such an affront go unchallenged and he prepared to lead a punitive expedition against Attica. Ferguson believes that it was on this occasion that the two Antigonid tribes were suppressed in Athens and their demes redistributed among the eleven remaining tribes.[2] Athens was obviously in need of allies. Her military forces, as we have already seen, were insufficient to enable her to wage war alone against Philip. Kephisodoros, who had succeeded Eurykleides and Mikion as leader of the city-state,[3] was sent on a mission to the Rhodians, the Cretan cities, Attalos and Ptolemy Epiphanes. There was no hope of help from the last; the others belonged to the Roman alliance, and it was through their intermediary that Athens became an ally of the great Italian city.

Athens as an ally of Rome

The situation in Athens was a difficult one at this time. A decree in honour of Kephisodoros[4] provides evidence that the city was short of wheat. As on every occasion when military operations were resumed in the Aegean, the problem of supplies became crucial. Did the Athenians then send an embassy to Rome? This question has been the subject of many controversies connected with the problem of Roman intervention in Greece. It is unlikely that a formal alliance existed between Athens and Rome before the Akarnanian incident.[5] How, then, are we to explain the presence of those Romans who, according to Polybios (XVI, xxv, 1) landed in the Piraeus shortly after the arrival of Attalos in the city? They were M. Claudius Nero, the victor of Metauros, Publius Sempronius Tuditanus, who had negotiated the peace of Phoinike, and M. Aemilius Lepidus. Had they come to Athens in response to a definite invitation from the Athenians, or, on the contrary, had the initiative come from certain circles in Rome which were anxious to be forearmed against any threat from the Aegean, and from a new Hannibal, by increasingly open intervention in Greek affairs?[6] According to the story that we have from Polybios, which stresses mainly the subservience of the Athenians towards Attalos (a twelfth tribe, named after him, was created at that time), the Roman ambassadors were careful not to intervene, merely escorting Attalos into the city; and only the Rhodian ambassadors were introduced into the Assembly, which had already listened to a letter from Attalos urging it to vote for war against Philip (Polybios XVI, xxv).

Attica was to be the principal victim of the first military operations. Philip twice invaded its territory, ravaging and destroying on a scale which further intensified the distress of the population. But finally the arrival of Roman reinforcements in the Piraeus, in the autumn of 200, forced the Macedonian king to withdraw. In Athens a sense of liberation prevailed, particularly as from this time onwards the main theatre of the war moved to the North. There were fresh displays of hostility towards Philip. The two 'Macedonian' tribes had already been suppressed, as we have seen. After the failure of Philip's latest venture against Attica, a decree was passed ordering the destruction of all the monuments, statues, dedications and so forth that had been set up in honour of the rulers of Philip's family.[7]

Livy (XXXI, 44) accuses the Athenians of having fought this war chiefly with words. Nevertheless the Piraeus, which served as home port for the allied fleet, was got ready for defence, as also were the frontier forts, since the Boiotians had come in on Philip's side. In other respects the Athenians appear to have played a not inconsiderable diplomatic role. In 198 they sent an embassy to the Achaeans urging them to abandon Philip. They were certainly present at the conference of Nikaia, and Kephisodoros went in person to Rome in 197 to take part in the peace negotiations (Polybios XVIII, 10) which followed the battle of Kynoscephalai. However, when Flamininus came to settle Greek affairs, the Athenians seem not to have obtained the hoped-for restoration of their island possessions, Lemnos, Imbros and Skyros.

The Second Macedonian war none the less marks the beginning of a close alliance between Athens and Rome, which Athenian policy during the war against Antiochos III was to make even closer. During the few years that followed the proclamation of Flamininus at the Isthmic Games, the laws laid down by Rome with increasing harshness had created a state of mind of which the Syrian king intended to take full advantage. Whereas everywhere in the city-states the rich supported Rome, the lower social strata were ready to welcome as liberator the Asiatic ruler whose prestige was constantly growing. The difficulties of supply, intensified by the presence of Roman troops, helped to exacerbate the situation. In Athens the 'pro-Roman' party then comprised such men as Mikion, son of Eurykleides, Diokles of Erchia, Echedemos of Kydathenaion and Leon of Aixone, who had real power firmly in their hands. But the news that Antiochos had landed in Greece aroused the hopes of those who resented Roman domination. Plutarch writes in the *Life of Cato*: 'Greece was at once a stormy sea of hopes and fears, being corrupted by her demagogues with expectations of royal bounty' (12). In Athens, a certain Apollodoros tried to stir up the *demos*, taking advantage of the presence in the city of Cato who was then military tribune in the army of the consul Manius Acilius (Livy XXXV, 50). But Flamininus intervened to restore order. Apollodoros was condemned to exile, while the Piraeus became the home port for the Roman fleet, as it had been during the war against Philip; and it was thanks to Acilius that the city's supplies, jeopardized by the landing of Antiochos at Chalkis, were safeguarded.

The Roman victory gave the control of the city to the men who had deliberately chosen a policy of alliance with Rome. These men, moreover, could delude themselves that they were giving Athens the role of arbiter in Greek affairs: thus it was a speech by Leon of Aixone before the Senate which persuaded the Romans to negotiate with the Aitolians (Polybios XXI, 31). The epigrams inscribed on the statues raised in their honour or on the rich tombs they had built for themselves speak volumes in this respect. Their names appear on coins. Furthermore, they constituted a kind of hereditary oligarchy: in 151 we find the grandson of Leon of Aixone holding the office that had been his grandfather's twenty years earlier. Nevertheless, and precisely in so far as the *demos* had lost all active role, save in exceptional circumstances, democratic institutions were still maintained. Even election by lot had been restored; but the magistracies had become increasingly expensive, and only the rich appeared on the lists, since they alone could afford the cost.

Athens was to remain loyal to the Roman alliance throughout the century. When the Third Macedonian war began, Athens stood almost alone by the side of Rome, whereas most other Greek states supported Perseus. This did not prevent the Roman generals from treating Athens in a high-handed fashion, requisitioning 100,000 *medimnai* of grain (Livy XLIII, 6). Although Athens was hard put to it to ensure her own supplies, she had to comply with the demand; but in 169 her ambassadors in Rome complained of the treatment she had received. This did not prevent the *demos* from voting a decree granting *proxenia* to Lucius Hortensius, who in 170 was in command of the Roman fleet (*I G* II² 907). In point of fact, after Pydna, Athens was one of the few Greek states to be favourably treated by the victor. The Athenian ambassadors in Rome demanded the reward of their loyalty, namely the restoration of Haliartos (Polybios XXX, 20), Delos and Lemnos. Athens may also have recovered Imbros and Skyros, which appear in her possession a few years later.[8] Imbros, Lemnos and Skyros remained cleruchies. Their inhabitants were Athenian citizens. There may perhaps have been fresh colonists, but most of the inhabitants of the three islands were descended from the fourth-century cleruchs and had preserved their demotic rights. Consequently their inclusion in the Athenian civic body could be effected without difficulty.

Inscriptions show that on the whole the administration of Athenian colonies remained the same as two centuries previously. Each cleruchy had its own assembly, its council and its magistrates, but its autonomy was purely relative, since it was controlled by magistrates from Athens. Thus at Delos and at Haliartos there were Athenian *epimeletes*, and the eponymous archon was an Athenian. At Salamis, Skyros, Imbros and Lemnos the Athenian magistrate was a *strategos*, in some cases assisted by a *hipparch* (at Lemnos and Salamis) and a treasurer of the public or of the military funds, while the eponymous archon was a local magistrate. Delos was rather a special case, for although the island formerly belonged to the Athenian empire, it had never included cleruchs. It was not until 166, after some of the island's inhabitants had been expelled, that a cleruchy was established there,[9] and Athenian priests replaced the Delian priests in all the sanctuaries.

The restoration of Athenian authority over certain Aegean islands and over Delos, and the Athenian claims to Oropos, did not fail to provoke disputes which the Romans were called upon to arbitrate. The Achaeans in particular took up the defence of the Delians, to whom they were bound by certain agreements (Polybios XXXII, 7). But the ever-increasing tension between Rome and the Achaean League proved profitable to the Athenians; and if they finally had to give up hopes of Oropos, they never paid the fine of five hundred talents—reduced to one hundred after the visit to Rome of the Academician Karneades—which had been imposed on them for having improperly invaded Boiotian territory.

The remarkable economic development of Delos [10] could not fail to affect Athens. However, the Athenian cleruchs formed only a small proportion of the island's population, which increased considerably during the thirty years that followed its association with Athens. Whereas to begin with they retained political control over the *polis*, they gradually came to lose this as increasingly autonomous ethnic groups took shape outside the political organization, the *Romaioi* being by far the most influential.

In Athens, meanwhile, there was an increasing display of support for Rome. A special rostrum had been set up close to the portico of Attalos, from which Roman magistrates or senators visiting Athens could address the people. A private residence had been built for them. *Epheboi* escorted them on their journeys. The flourishing schools of philosophy in Athens attracted young Romans seeking acquaintance with Greek culture, while not a year passed but some important magistrate from Rome came to make a stay in Athens.

Delos formed an additional link between Athens and Rome; and even after the cleruchy had been dissolved to make way for a *katoikia* of traditional Hellenistic type, grouping all the island's residents under the control of Athenian magistrates,[11] these links subsisted.

In other respects, the oligarchy which governed Athens sought to model the institutions of the *polis* on those of her great ally. Already at Delos the former magistrates' colleges had been replaced by new colleges copied from those of Rome, with dual powers at every grade. In Athens itself, the Areopagus was tending to become a Roman-style senate, and its functions developed at the expense of the people's courts and the *Boule* of the Six Hundred. Under the influence of a few devoted pro-Romans, such as Medeios of the Piraeus, Theodotos of Sounion, and Diodoros of Halai, all connected with the 'business world' of Delos,[12] a change in the constitution occurred during the last years of the century. W. S. Ferguson suggests [13] that this was connected with the revolt of the slaves in the Laurion mines which took place in 103/2, and with the presence in Athens of Marcus Antonius, on his way to the East where he was to attempt to crush the Cilician pirates. At all events, there was a definite shift in the constitution towards oligarchy. The people's courts were deprived of judicial control, appointment to the magistracy by lot was replaced by election, probably on a basis of limited franchise. It became possible to apply for and to hold the same office several times in succession, which up till then had been permitted only for highly specialized posts requiring technical qualifications, such as that of *strategos* or financial magistrate. This inevitably entailed a reduction in the size of the Areopagus and a more permanent membership. Were the powers of the old Council diminished thereby, as Ferguson suggests? [14] In point of fact, although power now belonged to a few influential families with Roman connections rather than to any constitutional body, the Areopagus tended more and more to identify itself with the Roman Senate and to claim the same honours and privileges. It undoubtedly retained control over weights and measures and over the coinage. At the same period, incidentally, a reform of weights and measures was entrusted to Diodoros of Halai.

Too little is known about the history of Athens during the years preceding her final struggle, but the decrees and the lists of magistrates betray the increasingly restricted character of the ruling oligarchy, to which the years of peace that Athens enjoyed under Roman domination had brought wealth and prosperity.

Society: intellectual and religious life in Athens during
the second century B.C.

We have unfortunately no documentary sources of information
about the second century comparable with those provided for the
preceding period by the fragments of the New Comedy.

There can be no doubt that the second century, particularly after
166, was a period of relative economic prosperity as compared with
the end of the previous century.[15] True, there were some critical
moments connected with supply difficulties in the early years of the
second century, in addition to the devastation inflicted by Philip on
the soil of Attica. But activity revived on the Piraeus, and foreigners
thronged there once again, grouped in religious or ethnic associations.
Athens then exported marble and also columns, capitals, vases,
bronze and silver vessels, and 'antiquities', which were increasingly
sought after by wealthy Romans. The workshops of Laurion were
once again in full swing. The new Athenian coinage was in wide
circulation, and in 189 Athens was able to lend the Aitolians, no
doubt on profitable terms, the indemnity which they owed to Rome.[16]
Mrs M. Thompson has shown in a recent article that, following the
battle of Kynoscephalai, Athens enjoyed a period of undeniable
prosperity, as is witnessed by the development of slave-labour not
only in industry but also in agriculture, on the large estates owned
by members of the ruling oligarchy.

This prosperity was further strengthened by the generous dona-
tions that came to Athens from certain Hellenistic courts. If the flow
of benefactions from the Ptolemies had somewhat slowed down,
owing to the difficulties then being experienced by the Egyptian
kingdom, the Attalids of Pergamon had taken on their role. Following the example of Attalos I at the end of the preceding century,
Eumenes II and Attalos II provided copious gifts. Eumenes raised a
huge portico on the south flank of the Acropolis, close to the sanctuary of Asklepios. Attalos proved even more generous than his
brother and presented the city with the famous portico which American archaeologists have recently reconstructed, standing on the east
side of the Agora. Finally, towards the middle of the century, at the
order of Antiochos IV, work was resumed on the Olympeion.[17]

This system of benefactions, moreover, was not practised solely by
kings. Gifts were also made by rich Athenian 'bourgeois', and this

clearly reflects the decline of the traditional *polis*. The liturgies of old were in fact a contribution to the common expenses, controlled and imposed by the *polis*. They formed part of a communal way of life, characteristic of the city-state from the sixth century onward. In the second century, on the contrary, the liturgies had disappeared, and the state assumed responsibility for public spending. But the generosity of rich individuals was displayed in the form of gifts intended both to enhance their own glory and to win them support, now that sortition had almost everywhere been replaced by election. Moreover, as we have seen, the magistracies had become expensive functions: more particularly the post of *agonothetes* or organizer of the games which were the indispensable corollary of the great religious festivals, now more numerous than ever. The cost of organizing these festivals fell partly on the exchequer of the city-state, but partly, too, on the magistrates elected for the purpose, who had inevitably to be wealthy men.

Where did their wealth come from? Unfortunately we lack the details which would enable us to specify the social condition of the men who now ruled the *polis*. However, it would seem that the process begun at the end of the fourth century had been accelerated. The ruling class was now composed of men who, besides owning land and deriving profit from it, were associated with the business world of which the Piraeus was still the centre, and were generally involved with the mining industry. They also had connections with the *negotiatores* of Delos. We need cite only two examples: that of Theodotus of Sounion, who was priest of Aphrodite at Delos and who urged the Athenians to award special honours to John Hyrkanos, ethnarch of Judaea; and that of Diodoros of Halai, who was *epimeletes* of the Piraeus and was chosen as *proxenos* by the foreign merchants of that port.

Moreover, while some of these men, Medeios for instance, belonged to the oldest Athenian families, others were of more dubious origin. In fact, the right of epigamy was now being more freely granted to foreigners, and they could contract legal marriages in this way.[18] The right of citizenship itself seems to have been granted with increasing liberality, and it is not unusual to find names of unmistakably foreign origin in the lists of magistrates. It is true that the growing cult of foreign deities may have encouraged certain Athenians to change their names, even to adopt a name suggestive of the god whose devotees they were. Thus we find Sarapion of Melite among the rulers of Athens at the end of the century. Among rich men of this class, who owed their fortunes in part to their support of alliance with Rome, old traditions tended to disappear, and there even seems to have been a certain degree of women's emancipation. This should not be exaggerated, however, and a recent study has shown that in the Hellenistic epoch 'the existence of women had scarcely changed since the time of Xenophon, even since that of Homer: spinning, weaving, supervising the work of slaves, such were the daily tasks of the housewife and she was allowed no outside activity'.[19] The same study shows, however, that 'the most acceptable pretext for women to go outside their homes was the religious pretext'.[20] This was nothing new; already in the days of Aristophanes, the *Thesmophoriai* had provided women with such an opportunity. But in third-century and even more in second-century Athens, there was an increase in the number of religious associations which included Athenians and foreigners, women and slaves. True, the movement developed slowly at first, and up till the middle of the second century few Athenians belonged to the associations dedicated to the worship of any foreign deity, except for those officially admitted to the civic pantheon, such as Bendis or Asklepios. At the end of the third century, however, the number of religious associations increased, and in the second century the barriers which prevented foreigners from entering the *orgeones*, and Athenians from joining the groups that worshipped alien deities, tended to drop. Among the most venerated of these deities we must include the Great Mother of Pessinonte, whose worship, with its bloodthirsty rites, was probably introduced by Attalos of Pergamon at the end of the third century. These associations, indeed, seem to have been connected with the worship of older and more traditional deities: for instance the Dionysiac *thiasoi*, which tended to become associations of professional actors responsible for organizing festivals and games.

The traditional gods were by no means neglected, but their cult was chiefly the occasion for festivals and for theatrical performances and games. To the traditional festivals—the Dionysia, the Panathenaia—were now added festivals in honour of the Hellenistic kings who had protected Athens, Ptolemaia and Attaleia. Here too we witness the growth of professionalism, among both athletes and actors, and these festivals tended increasingly to become spectacles offered to a passive audience of citizens and of those foreigners who were still drawn to Athens by the memory of her past greatness.

Of these, the most important were those who came to listen to the teaching of Athenian philosophers. The most remarkable personality of that time was Karneades, who had succeeded Arkesilaos at the head of the Academy. He was to play a considerable part as ambassador to the Romans. His pragmatic, eclectic teaching, in strong contrast with the dogmatism of the Stoics, then led by Diogenes, inevitably appealed to the Romans. After him, Klitomachos and Philo helped to introduce into Rome a Platonism that was far removed from its original form. The Stoic school was to enjoy renewed success with Panaitios of Rhodes, who was also to play an important part in bringing Greek philosophy to Rome.

The Peripatetic and Epicurean schools were less prominent at this time. The former was represented by Kritolaos, who accompanied Karneades and Diogenes to Rome. The latter, which tended to remain in the background because the Epicurean sage was above all a private man, did not attain any great brilliance in second-century Athens. All these schools, except that of the 'Garden', had now become institutions under the protection of the *polis*, and every young Athenian of good family, after serving as an ephebe, was bound to attend them, studying under the great teachers of the day and making friends with distinguished foreigners, sons of Asiatic kings or of Roman senators, who had come to seek initiation into Greek culture, of which Athens remained the unchallenged centre.[21]

The final struggle

This picture of Athenian life in the second century is perhaps misleading. Athens was certainly prosperous, she had enjoyed three-quarters of a century of peace, she attracted many foreigners and her philosophical schools were justly renowned. But all this concerned only a tiny minority. Unfortunately, we have no information about the rest of the population, the mass of poor citizens who, as in the past, made a scanty living from the produce of their land or of their craftsmanship. Texts and inscriptions acquaint us only with the minority of rich and influential men who governed the *polis*. The others remain hidden in total darkness. They were to emerge from this suddenly on a summons from the King of Pontos, Mithridates Eupator.

Relations between Athens and the Graeco-barbarian kingdoms of the Black Sea were of long standing. They were bound up essentially with Athens' need to procure wheat, and from the fourth century onwards decrees in honour of the rulers of the Bosphoros reflect a concern to win the favour of these princes, on whom the city-state depended partly for her food supplies. The kingdom of Pontos had broken away relatively soon from the Seleucid kingdom. The reigning dynasty was of Iranian origin, but was strongly Hellenized.[22] In the first half of the century Athens had formed close relations with Pharnaces, and she maintained them under that prince's successors. Shortly before 110/9 a monument had been dedicated to Mithridates Eupator by an Athenian magistrate at Delos.[23]

Meanwhile, however, the King of Pontos had succeeded in laying hold of all the northern part of Asia Minor, and now threatened the Roman province there.[24] His hostility towards Rome was at first covert and interspersed with truces, but from 90/89 onwards the breach was an open one. Italy was then passing through a period of crisis, under cover of which the King of Pontos succeeded in gaining control over the whole of Asia.

He was acclaimed as a liberator by the Greeks of Asia, and also by those of Europe. All who found the Roman yoke intolerable turned to him as their saviour. An obscure philosopher of the Peripatetic school, Athenion, who had been sent as delegate to the Pontic ruler, sent back to Athens letters announcing the imminent landing of the King, and a promise that Athens would have her democracy restored and her debts cancelled, and that the Athenians would be copiously rewarded by the King. As we may well imagine, such promises were enthusiastically welcomed by the mass of the population, who saw only the disadvantages of peaceful relations with Rome. The return of Athenion was the signal for a democratic revolution which forced the oligarchic leaders to fly the country, while the philosopher assumed plenary powers with the title of *strategos* of the hoplites, and democratic institutions were, in theory, restored. Poseidonios has recorded the triumphal return of Athenion:[25]

> ... as he entered the city, almost everybody flooded out in a crush to receive him. Some, indeed, went simply as spectators in amazement at the chance which brought back to Athens in a silver-footed litter and purple wraps an impostor who had never seen so much as a

streak of purple in his beggar's rags; for not even a Roman had ever paraded in such a haughty fashion in Attica. Accordingly men, women and children thronged hastily to see the sight, naturally expecting great things from Mithridates, seeing that this pauper, Athenion, who had made his living by subscription lectures, had come back from his court in grand estate, lolling along at his ease through country and town. Out came the Dionysiac artists, too, with the request that the envoy of the new Dionysos (for such was the rank and title of Mithridates among the Olympians) should be their guest, and accept their vows and thanksgivings. And so it came that he who had departed from a mean little hired flat was entertained on his return in the house of the Delian nabob, Dies, a palace rich with rugs and paintings, statues and silver plate. . . . Next day throngs of people assembled at his house, waiting for him to come out, and the Kerameikos was packed with citizens and foreigners who, without the formality of a summons, rushed pell-mell to hold a town meeting. Athenion had difficulty in making his way forward; for around and in front of him was a bodyguard of politicians who wished to stand in with a popular movement, and who strove to touch though it were only the hem of his garment. At length he reached the platform which had been built before the stoa of Attalos for the use of the Roman generals, and mounting on it, he looked upon the multitude all about him. . . .

and addressed them. His speech related the triumphs of Mithridates, the extent of his powers, the welcome he had received in Greek cities; it concluded with an appeal:

Let us not put up with the anarchy which the Roman senate is prolonging till it has ascertained how we ought to be governed. Let us not stand by inactive while the temples are shut, the *gymnasia* foul through disuse, the theatre without the ekklesia, the jury-courts silent, and the Pnyx taken away from the people, though consecrated to its use by the oracles of the gods. Let us not stand by inactive, men of Athens, whilst the sacred cry Iacchos is silenced, the hallowed sanctuary of Castor and Pollux is closed, and the conference halls of the philosophers are voiceless.

Then the crowd, Poseidonios relates, acclaimed him and appointed him general of the hoplites.

While these events were taking place in Athens, Mithridates had sent Apellikon of Teos to seize Delos.[26] The failure of this attempt may perhaps account for the fall of the philosopher Athenion; for in the ensuing months we hear no mention of him. When Sulla came to besiege Athens it was one Aristion, also a philosopher but of the Epicurean school, who now ruled the city-state. It has been suggested that the same man may have been called Athenion by Poseidonios and Aristion by Plutarch,[27] for the same tyrannical measures are attributed to both of them: the confiscation of property, the imprisonment and even execution of those suspected of pro-Roman sympathies. The argument put forward by Ferguson against this identification is that Plutarch refers to a number of tyrants in Athens (*Life of Sulla*, 13). There is no proof, however, that Plutarch was referring to the period preceding Aristion's accession to power.

In any case, when Sulla began the siege of Athens, Aristion's tyranny became harsher, and, moreover, the city, being cut off from the Piraeus and deprived of supplies, experienced dramatic hardships: 'a bushel of wheat sold in the city for a thousand drachmas . . . men made food for themselves of the *parthenion* (feverfew) which grew on the Acropolis, and boiled down shoes and leather oil-flasks to eat' (ibid.). Meanwhile Sulla brought up fresh battering-rams and had no hesitation in plundering sanctuaries and cutting down the sacred grove of the Academy to rebuild the engines that had been destroyed. Yet when the city was in such dire straits that Aristion finally decided to negotiate, Sulla would not listen; and he entered Athens by a surprise attack.

> Sulla . . . led his army into the city at midnight. The sight of him was made terrible by blasts of many trumpets and bugles, and by the cries and yells of the soldiery now let loose by him for plunder and slaughter, and rushing through the narrow streets with drawn swords. There was therefore no counting of the slain, but their numbers are to this day determined only by the space that was covered with blood. For without mention of those who were killed in the rest of the city, the blood that was shed in the market-place covered all the Kerameikos inside the Dipylon gate; nay, many say that it flowed through the gate and deluged the suburb. But although those who were thus slain were so many, there were yet more who slew themselves, out of yearning pity for their native city, which they thought was going to be destroyed. For this conviction made the best of them give up in despair and fear to survive, since they

expected no humanity or moderation in Sulla. However, partly at the instance of the exiles Meidias and Kalliphon, who threw themselves at his feet in supplication, and partly because all the Roman senators who were in his following interceded for the city, being himself also by this time sated with vengeance, after some words in praise of the ancient Athenians, he said that he forgave a few for the sake of many, the living for the sake of the dead (Plutarch, *Life of Sulla*, 14).

The Piraeus still held out, however, and so did the Acropolis, where Aristion had taken refuge. Curion succeeded in taking the Acropolis, while Sulla pursued the army of Mithridates into Boiotia. After his victory at Chaironea, he returned to besiege the Piraeus, which surrendered. He burnt down the fortified outworks which protected the port and the famous arsenal built by Philon in the fourth century.[28]

Athens was doomed. When he returned to the city in 84 B.C. Sulla gave her back Delos, which had been declared free two years previously; but the island, too, had now begun to decline, and in a world dominated by Rome such a possession now proved but an empty compensation.

The democratic constitution re-established in 89/8 had been suppressed once again, and power vested in a docile oligarchy without real authority. Out of regard for her past, Athens was allowed to remain a free city; but she had finally renounced any suggestion of independence.

Soon afterwards, the defeat and death of Mithridates brought an end to what had been the last resurgence of Hellenism. The shadow of Rome now stretched over the entire Mediterranean.

Conclusion

To study the decline of any civilization is always a tempting prospect for the historian; it is one way of understanding the processes of history through a chosen example. The decline of Athens is a singularly fascinating story. The ancient writers were aware of this: first Plato, then Aristotle and the Stoics, finally Polybios and Cicero examined the development and the destiny of the *polis*. Today's historian has the advantage of distance, but at the same time he is liable to apply contemporary preoccupations to the reality of the past. Every sort of factor has been adduced by way of explanation: moral crisis, religious crisis, economic and social crisis, the internal contradictions of the slave-labour system; and all contain a partial truth, but none explains that whole which is the *polis*. The concept of the *polis* was, originally, that of a community of free men, living in perfect autarchy under the protection of the gods and defending themselves against any attack from outside. Needless to say, this ideal concept was never realized at any moment in Greek history, for very soon, and at a very early stage, the need for supplies of grain and common metals imposed upon the Greeks a system of relations which implied division of labour, slavery and social inequality. The history of Athens is typical in this respect, since as early as the sixth century B.C. she found herself involved in a complex system of relations, which hastened her evolution towards democracy, a democracy that presupposed slavery and the exploitation of her Aegean allies. From that moment, the apogee of Athens contained within itself the elements of her decline. Deprived of her allies, Athens was condemned to provide for herself the resources which would enable democracy to survive and to protect itself; and to accomplish this she must give up the traditional ethic of the *polis*, that autarchy of which some theorists were still dreaming in the fourth century, and to seek an opening on to the outside world, to develop her industry by a large-scale recourse to slave-labour, to attract foreign traders and integrate them into the civic community. A few men, towards the middle of the fourth century, were intuitively aware of this new necessity. But there were too many obstacles to its fulfilment, some due to the very structure of the essentially rural civic society, others to the general conditions of the Aegean world, to the threat from Macedon and, later, to the great upheavals caused by the conquest of Alexander, and others again to the political regime itself, to that democracy which had constituted the greatness of Athens and which now doomed her to die. Not, indeed, in the way that, half a century ago, some scholars believed who overstressed the excesses of demagogy and the ignorance of the masses; but because true democracy presupposes a state of social equilibrium which can only be realized in a world that is still primitive, or in a future socialist world; and because it presupposes, too, a profound change within man himself, as fourth-century Athenians had intuitively felt with their high regard for education, *paideia*. All things considered, it is perhaps this intuitive awareness of the real problems and the impossibility of solving them which, across the gulf of time, gives such rare value to the history of the decline of Athens.

Abbreviations

Journals

ABSA	*Annual of the British School at Athens*
AC	*Antiquité Classique*
ANS-MN	*American Numismatic Society—Museum Notes*
BCH	*Bulletin de Correspondance Hellénique*
JHS	*Journal of Hellenic Studies*
PP	*La Parola del Passato*
REA	*Revue des Études Anciennes*
REG	*Revue des Études Grecques*
RH	*Revue Historique*
RP	*Revue de Philologie*
TAPA	*Transactions of the American Philological Association*

Books

IG	*Inscriptiones Graecae*
OGIS	*Orientis Graeci Inscriptiones Selectae*
Syll.[3]	Dittenberger, *Sylloge Inscriptionum Graecarum*, 3rd edition

Notes

Chapter 1 Athens after the end of the Peloponnesian war

1 Xenophon, *Hellenica*, II, 30, 11; Lysias, *Against Eratosthenes*, 72 ff.
2 On the meaning of this expression during the closing years of the fifth century, cf. A. Fuks, *The Ancestral Constitution*, London, 1953; Sergio A. Cecchin, *Patrios politeia. Un tentativo propagandistico durante la guerra del Peloponneso*, Turin, 1969; and more recently M. I. Finley, *The Ancestral Constitution*, Cambridge, 1971.
3 Xenophon, *Hellenica*, II, 5, 15; cf. *Athenaion Politeia*, 36, 2.
4 Cf. *Ath. Pol.*, 40, 2.
5 Cf. in particular the estimates of W. Gomme, *The Population of Athens in the Fifth and Fourth Centuries B.C.*, 1953.
6 Xenophon, *Memorabilia*, II, 7, 11; 8, 1–3.
7 Xenophon, *Oeconomicus*, XX, 26.
8 Cf. in particular M. I. Finley, *Studies in Land and Credit in Ancient Athens* (500–200 B.C.). *The Horoi Inscriptions*, 1952.
9 Andokides, *On the Peace*, 36.
10 On the problem of these internal conflicts in Athens at the beginning of the century, see C. Mossé, *La Fin de la Démocratie Athénienne*, Paris, 1962, pp. 147 ff.; 287 ff.
11 This, at any rate, is what emerges from the argument of Dionysios of Halikarnassos in Lysias' 34th speech, against the decree proposed by a member of the moderate party, Phormisios, seeking to confine the *politeia* to owners of property.
12 Diels, frag. 25, quoted by T. A. Sinclair, *History of Greek Political Thought*, London, 1967, p. 256.
13 The bibliography on Socrates is so extensive that it cannot be cited here. The reader is referred to A. J. Festugière, *Socrate*, 1966 (2nd edition), and to the section on Socrates in V. Ehrenberg's *From Solon to Socrates*, London, 1968, pp. 362 ff.; also for an interpretation of the trial, see C. Mossé, *Histoire d'une Démocratie: Athènes*, 1971, pp. 107–10.

Chapter 2 The rebirth of imperialist democracy (404–359 B.C.)

1 *Ath. Pol.*, 41, 2.
2 Thucydides, VIII, 97.

3 Lysias, *Against Nikomachos*, 4.
4 *Ath. Pol.*, 41.
5 Cf. above, p. 12.
6 On the question of the political character of the Athenian army in the Classical period, see C. Mossé 'Armée et cité grecque', *REA*, lxv (1963), 190–297; 'Le rôle de l'armée dans la révolution de 411 à Athènes', *RH*, (1964), 1–10.
7 These problems as a whole are analysed in C. Mossé, *La Fin de la Démocratie Athénienne*, pp. 273 ff.; 313 ff.; cf. also 'Le rôle politique des armées dans le monde grec à la fin de l'époque classique', *Problèmes de la guerre en Grèce ancienne*, ed. J. P. Vernand, Paris, 1968, pp. 221 ff.
8 On this question cf. Rudi Thomsen, *Eisphora, A study of direct taxation in ancient Athens*, Copenhagen, 1964, pp. 24 ff.; 194 ff.
9 'Callistratos of Aphidna and his contemporaries', *Historia*, v (1956), 178–203 (*Essays in Greek politics*, pp. 123 ff.).
10 *On the Peace*, 36
11 Cf. in particular the clauses of the treaty of alliance between Athens, the Arcadians, the Achaeans, the Eleans and the Phliasians, *Syll.*³ 181.
12 *IG* II² 43 = *Syll.*³ 147.
13 On the powers of the *synedrion* of the allies see C. Mossé, *Institutions grecques*, pp. 124 ff., where the principal texts are quoted.
14 Cf. in particular *IG* II² 125 = *Syll.*³ 191.
15 On the political role of Chares cf. J. de Romilly, 'Les modérés Athéniens vers le milieu du IVe siècle', *REG*, lxii (1954), 323–33, particularly 327.
16 On the reorganization of the Laurion mines in the fourth century, see particularly the article by M. Crosby, 'The leases of the Laurion mines', *Hesperia*, xix (1950), 189–312; cf. also R. J. Hopper, 'The Attic silver mines in the fourth century B.C.', *ABSA*, xlviii (1953), 200–54; 'The Laureion mines: a reconsideration', ibid. (1968), 293–325.
17 *Ath. Pol.*, 47, 1.
18 For instance R. J. Hopper in his 1953 article, p. 238.
19 Cf. S. Lauffer, 'Prosopographische Bemerkungen zu den attischen Grübenpachtlisten', *Historia*, vi (1957), 287–305.
20 Cf. the examples quoted by P. Gauthier, 'Symbola, les étrangers et la justice dans les cités grecques', pp. 1–16 ff.
21 Cf. the article by Louis Gernet, 'Sur les actions commerciales en droit athénien', *REG* (1938) (*Droit et Société dans la Grèce ancienne*, pp. 173 ff.).
22 Cf. the recent study by J. Pečirka, *The Formula for the Grant of enktesis in Attic Inscriptions*, Prague, 1966.

Chapter 3 The conflict with Macedonia (359–337 B.C.)

1 There are many studies of Philip of Macedon, which are not always impartial, modern critics having frequently adopted the partisan attitudes of antiquity. One of the most discerning is that of A. Momigliano, *Filippo il Macedone*, 1934. The reader may also consult P. Cloché, *Un fondateur d'empire, Philippe II roi de Macédoine*, 1955.

2 For detailed knowledge of these events, the reader should consult those works of general history which make ample use of the writings of Demosthenes and Aeschines and also of the account by Diodoros. On the character of the peace of 346, see Momigliano, op. cit. pp. 493 ff.; J. T. Griffith, 'The so-called *koine eirene* of 346 B.C.', *JHS* (1939), 71–9; on the role of the Delphic Amphiktyonia as guarantor of that peace, see M. Sordi, 'La fondation du collège des Naopes et le renouveau politique de l'amphictyonie au IVe siècle', *BCH*, lxxxi, 1957, 38–75.

3 Modern writers tend to adopt as passionate an attitude towards Demosthenes as towards Philip, approval of the one inevitably implying criticism of the other. In France, Cloché's book, *Demosthène et la Fin de la Démocratie Athénienne*, 1937, is an impassioned tribute to the orator. Anglo-Saxon historians are more cautious, Germans frankly hostile. Here again, it is impossible to give a full bibliography. Consult general histories and the prefaces to the latest editions of the speeches of Demosthenes.

4 On these controversies see the article by R. Sealey, 'Athens after the Social War', *JHS*, lxxv (1955), 74–81 (*Essays in Greek Politics*, pp. 164–82).

5 Cf. Demosthenes, XXII, 48, 49; XX, 127, XXIV, 11.

6 *I G* II², 1613, l. 302.

7 *Against Timocrates*, 154; *Against Leptines*, 48; 49; 161.

8 On the evolution of Isokrates' thought and the role attributed by him to Philip, cf. Mossé, *La Fin de la Démocratie Athénienne*, pp. 439 ff.

9 *Against Philippides*, 1.

10 *On the Chersonese*, 40–1.

11 See Mossé, *La Fin de la Démocratie Athénienne*, pp. 362 ff. for references to the texts quoted or commented on throughout this section.

12 Cf. in particular L. Gernet's introduction to the *Belles Lettres* edition, Paris, 1951, pp. 94 ff.

13 On the development of monarchical theories in Athens in the fourth century, see Mossé, *La Fin de la Démocratie Athénienne*, pp. 375 ff.

14 Cf. A. Aymard, 'L'institution monarchique', *Relazioni del X Congresso Internazionale di Scienze Storiche*, vol. II, *Storia dell' Antichità*, Rome, 1955, pp. 215–34 (*Études d'Histoire Ancienne*, Paris, 1967, pp. 123 ff.).

15 Cf. Plutarch, *Life of Phokion*, 14.

16 For an account of military operations and an analysis of diplomatic relations, see general histories of Greece. I have attempted here only to show the two conflicting trends in Greek public opinion, expressed in Demosthenes' *On the Crown* on the one hand, and in Aeschines' *Against Ktesiphon* on the other.

17 Cf. Lykourgos, *Against Leokrates*, 37; Hypereides, frag. 29 (Jensen).

18 Cf. Lykourgos, *Against Leokrates*, 41: 'Many sufferings were being visited upon the city; every citizen had felt misfortune at its worst; but the sight which would most surely have stirred the onlooker and moved him to tears over the sorrows of Athens was to see the people vote that slaves should be released, that aliens should become

Athenians and the disfranchised regain their rights: the nation that once proudly claimed to be indigenous and free.' Thus, while giving approval to the measures of public safety proposed by Hypereides, Lykourgos none the less considered them disastrous.

19 In this respect the difference between the attitude of a man like Hypereides and the remarks of Lykourgos quoted above is highly significant. In the second speech against Aristogeiton, Demosthenes merely alludes to the decree about the *atimoi* and defends it warmly.

20 Demosthenes, *Against Aristogeiton*, II, 11.

21 Plutarch, *Life of Phokion*, 16.

22 Much has been written about the League of Corinth. The peace terms are partially known through an extremely mutilated inscription (*I G* II² 236 = *Syll.*³ 260) which has been the subject of numerous commentaries. For the bibliography and the various problems raised by this text, cf. Mossé, *La Fin de la Démocratie Athénienne*, pp. 464 ff.

23 This decree was published for the first time by B. Meritt (*Hesperia* xxi (1952), 355–9). See the commentary on it by M. Ostwald, 'The Athenian legislation against tyranny and subversion', *TAPA*, lxxxvi (1955), 103–28; cf. also J. Pouilloux, *Choix d'inscriptions grecques*, Paris, 1960, no. 32, pp. 121 ff.; and Mossé, 'A propos de la loi d'Eucrates sur la tyrannie', *Eirene*, viii (1970), 71–8.

24 Ibid., 75–6.

Chapter 4 Athens at the time of Alexander

1 This is the title retained by most modern scholars; it appears in a fragment of Hypereides; cf. G. Colin, 'Note sur l'administration financière de l'orateur Lycurgue', *REA*, xxx (1928), 189–200. The office appears to have been conferred on him as an exceptional measure for four years, then renewed later.

2 This decree has come down to us in two forms: (a) a fragmentary inscription (*I G* II² 457 = *Syll.*³ 326) and (b) a text appended to his *Life of Lykourgos* by the pseudo-Plutarch. Cf. the French edition of Lykourgos in the *Collection des Universités de France*, pp. 7 ff. where both texts are translated.

3 *I G* II², 333–4; 739–41.

4 *I G* II², 351.

5 *I G* II², 807–9.

6 Cf. Stratokles' decree, pseudo-Plutarch, *Life of Lykourgos*.

7 Cf. C. Pelekides, *Histoire de l'éphébie attique des origines à 31 av. J.-G.*, Paris, 1960.

8 On Harpalos, the latest study is by E. Badian, *JHS* 1961. See also G. Colin, 'Demosthène et l'affaire d'Harpale', *REG*, xxxviii, 306–49; xxxix (1926), 31–89; 'Le discours d'Hypéride sur l'argent d'Harpale', *Annales de l'Est, Mémoires*, no. 4, 1934; and the same author's introduction to Hypereides' *Against Demosthenes* in the *Belles Lettres* edition, Paris, 1946, pp. 221 ff.

9 Plutarch, *Life of Phokion*.
10 Cf. A. Aymard, 'Un ordre d'Alexandre', *REA*, xxxix (1937), pp. 5–28.
11 Cf. G. Mathieu, 'Notes sur Athènes à la veille de la guerre Lamiaque', *RP*, lv (1929), 159–83.
12 G. Colin, preface to Hypereides' *Against Demosthenes*, p. 324.
13 On the rise in prices and the speculation in which certain landowners engaged, cf. the speech *Against Phainippos* (pseudo-Demosthenes).
14 Demosthenes, XXXIV, 8.
15 Ibid. 36.
16 Demosthenes, LVI, 10.
17 Demosthenes, XLII, 3; 21; 31.
18 Cf. the latest study, G. E. M. de Ste Croix, 'The estate of Phainippus', *Ancient Society and Institutions, Studies presented to V. Ehrenberg*, Oxford, 1966, pp. 109 ff. which includes a bibliography of earlier work.
19 *Collection des Universités de France*, pp. 77, 21.
20 *I G* II², 1580; 1954; 1958; 1602; etc. Cf. the paper by D. N. Lewis, *The Athenian Rationes Centesimae*, presented at the colloquium held at Royaumont in September 1969, to be published.
21 Cf. Hopper, in *ABSA*, xlviii (1953), 251–2.
22 Hypereides, *For Euxenippos*, 1.
23 For an analysis of the sources referring to Leosthenes and the preparation for the Lamian war, cf. G. Mathieu, op. cit. (n. 11) and especially E. Lepore, 'Leostene e le origini della guerra lamiaca', *PP*, xl, ii (1955), 161 ff.
24 *Life of Phokion*, 24 ff.
25 Ibid., 28.
26 XVIII, 18, 4.

Chapter 5 The period of Diadochoi

1 The main facts and the problems they raise are set out, together with the latest bibliography, in E. Will, *Histoire Politique du Monde Hellénistique (323–30 av. J.-C.)*, 2 vols, Nancy, 1966–7.
2 The history of Athens in the Hellenistic period is studied at length by W. S. Ferguson, *Hellenistic Athens, an Historical Essay*, London, 1911. Since the publication of this book a number of special studies have appeared, publishing the results of the excavations undertaken by the French School at Delos and also epigraphical documents. Problems of chronology, in particular, have given rise to a number of controversies. Ferguson's book, however, remains reliable on many points and we shall frequently refer to it.
3 For this chapter see Mossé, *La Tyrannie dans la Grèce Antique*, Paris, 1969, pp. 155 ff.
4 XVIII, 56. On the interpretation of Polyperchon's policy cf. Heuss, 'Antigonos Monophthalmos und die griechischen Städte', *Hermes*, lxxiii (1938), 142 ff.

Notes

5 Cf. P. Cloché, 'Remarques sur la politique d'Antigone le Borgne à l'égard des cités grecques', *AC*, xvii (1948), 101 ff.; A. H. Simpson, 'Antigonos the One-Eyed and the Greeks', *Historia*, viii (1959), 385 ff.

6 Cf. Ferguson, op. cit. p. 471; Will, op. cit. I, p. 63.

7 Cf. the most recent study, L. C. Smith, 'Demochares of Leukonoe and the dates of his exile', *Historia*, xi (1962), 114 ff.

8 Cf. *I G* II², 463, decree entrusting Demochares with the task of repairing the fortifications of Athens.

9 On the League of 302, cf. the famous decree of Epidaurus, *I G* IV, I, 68, which has already been the subject of a number of commentaries; see particularly F. Hampl, *Die Griechische Staatsverträge des 4. Jahr. v. Chr.*, Leipzig, 1938, pp. 59–61; 113 ff.; Ferguson, 'Demetrios Poliorcetes and the Hellenic League', *Hesperia* (1948), 112 ff.; L. Robert, 'Adeimantos et la Ligue de Corinthe', *Hellenica*, ii (1946), 15 ff.; G. Daux, 'Adeimantos de Lampsaque et le renouvellement de la ligue de Corinthe par Demetrios Poliorcete', *Mélanges Oikonomos* (1955), pp. 241 ff.

10 On the relations maintained by Athens at this time with the opponents of Poliorketes, cf. *Syll.*³ 362; 374; cf. also M. Fortuna, *Cassandro, re di Macedonia*, 1965, pp. 111 ff.

11 For Athenian society after 350 and the changes that took place in it see Mossé, *La Fin de la Démocratie Athénienne*, pp. 133 ff. The difference between the peasants of Aristophanes, impoverished by the war but still controlling the destiny of the *polis*, and the rich landowners depicted by Menander, is particularly eloquent.

12 On the development of Athenian trade at the end of the fourth century, see Rostovtzeff, *The Social and Economic History of the Hellenistic World*, pp. 60 ff.; 1349 ff.

13 Cf. above, p. 145.

14 Kallipides in Menander's *Dyskolos* gives a dowry of three talents to his daughter; the daughter of Smikrines in the *Epitrepontes* has a dowry of four talents.

15 On this point, cf. the recent study of C. Vatin, *Recherches sur le mariage et la condition de la femme mariée à l'époque hellénistique*, 1970.

16 On this point, valuable information will be found in J. Pečirka's study, *The Formula for the Grant of Enktesis in Attic Inscriptions*, Prague, 1966.

17 Cf. Mossé, *La Fin de la Démocratie Athénienne*, p. 181 and n. 5 for the latest bibliography on this question.

18 *I G* II² 1553–1578. W. Gomme, *The Population of Athens in the Fifth and Fourth Centuries, B.C.*, 1953, p. 41, n. 2, estimates the number at some fifty per annum.

Chapter 6 The final upsurge of nationalism: the Chremonidean war. Athens loses her independence and her political importance

1 Ferguson, *Hellenistic Athens*, pp. 126 ff.; on Lachares, see the article by de Sanctis, 'Lacare', *Rivista de Filologia*, n.s. vi (1928), pp. 59 ff., and

the same author's 'Atene dopo Ipso e un papiro fiorentino', ibid. xiv (1936), 134–52; 253–73.

2 On the date of Athens' surrender to Demetrios, cf. *I G* II² 646.

3 On the adventures of Demetrios after Ipsos, see Will, *Histoire Politique du Monde Hellénistique*, pp. 71 ff., where the main problems are discussed and the appropriate bibliographical references given.

4 Ferguson, op. cit. p. 152, n. 4. Cf. Will, op. cit. pp. 189; 194; R. Flacelière, *Les Aetoliens à Delphes*, 1937, pp. 84; 190, which suggests certain qualifications to the views of Tarn, *Antigonos Gonatas*, 1933.

5 The phrase is used by Will, op. cit. p. 93.

6 For this aspect of Gonatas' policy see Tarn, op. cit. pp. 233 ff. His view is perhaps too 'idyllic' (Will, op. cit. p. 189), but the personality of Gonatas has undoubted fascination. Cf. F. Sartori, 'Cremonide: un dissidio fra politica e filosofia', *Miscellanea di Studi Alessandrini in memoria di A. Rostagni*, Turin, 1963.

7 Cf. Fellmann, *Antigonos Gonatas und die griechischen Staaten*, Wurzburg, 1930, pp. 26 ff.; 47 ff.

8 The dating of the decree raises extremely complex problems. See Tarn, 'The new dating of the Chremonidean War', *JHS* liv (1934), 26 ff.; Sartori, op. cit. p. 118, n. 5, for the latest statement of the question.

9 It will be noticed that the appeal to the ancestral constitution, which formed the central theme of the political propaganda of the oligarchs at the end of the fifth and in the fourth centuries, is here taken up by men who claim to stand for democracy in opposition to the domination of Macedon and to its supporters. This ambiguity is discussed by M. I. Finley—who incidentally does not cite the decree of Chremonides— in *The Ancestral Constitution, an Inaugural Lecture*, Cambridge, 1971.

10 The first mention of the 'Chremonidean' war is found in Hegesandros (ap. Ath. VI, 250 ff.), the author of *Hypomnemata* (of which Plutarch makes use), living in the second century B.C.

11 See note 6.

12 Whose name occurs in Chremonides' decree. There is a copious bibliography on this problem. See the discussion in Will, op. cit. I, pp. 198–9.

13 Rostovtzeff puts forward the economic argument (I, pp. 215 ff.) which is also found in Tarn, op. cit. pp. 219 ff.), but in order to explain Athens' interest in maintaining links with Egypt. On the economic aims of Ptolemaic policy in the Aegean, cf. Will, op. cit. pp. 159 ff.

14 Cf. Will, op. cit. p. 199 for evidence of the Spartan king's prestige.

15 Cf. Sartori, op. cit. p. 144, n. 122. The decree was passed at a meeting of the people's Assembly presided over by Sostratos, son of Kallistratos of Erchia.

16 Cf. E. Vanderpool, J. R. MacCredie and A. Steinberg, 'Koroni: a Ptolemaic camp on the east coast of Attica', *Hesperia*, xxxi (1962), 26 ff.; xxxiii (1964), 69 ff.

17 On the problems raised by the battle of Kos, cf. Will, op. cit, I, p. 201.

18 Cf. in particular J. Pouilloux, 'Antigonos Gonatas et Athènes après la

guerre de Chremonides', *BCH*, lxx (1946), 488 ff., and the observations
of Will, op. cit., I, p. 205.
19 On Philochoros, cf. the introduction by Jacoby, *Die Fragmente der
griechischen Historiker*, III, b, no. 328, pp. 220 ff. *Atthis*, 107 ff.
20 Quoted by Sinclair, *History of Greek Political Thought*, p. 256.
21 Cf. Diogenes Laertius, VII, 6 ff.
22 Cf. *Syll.*³ 454—decree of the people of Salamis in honour of
Herakleitos.
23 On Aratos' operations against Athens cf. Feyel, *Polybe et l'histoire de
la Béotie au IIIe siècle*, 1942, p. 98, and n. 1.
24 Cf. the honorific decree, *Syll.*³ 497.
25 On the problems raised by the 'liberation' of Athens and its attitude
towards the Achaean League and Aratos, cf. Will, op. cit. I, pp. 329–30.
26 On this point, see, however, M. Thompson, *The New Style Silver
Coinage of Athens*, 1961, proposing the date 196/5 for the appearance
of this new coinage in preference to the generally accepted date 229/8.
27 Cf. Pečirka, *The Formula for the Grant of enktesis in Attic Inscriptions*,
pp. 96 ff.
28 On the changes taking place in Athens and in Athenian interests during
the last third of the third century, see Ferguson, op. cit. pp. 237 ff.
29 For a general study of the problem of Doson's policy towards the
Greek city-states and the formation of the Hellenic League, cf. Will,
op. cit. I, pp. 354 ff. and notes.
30 It was at this time that the Ptolemaia were celebrated in Athens and
the Ptolemaion gymnasium was founded. On this last point, however,
see M. Thompson, 'Ptolemy Philometor and Athens', *ANS-MN* xi
(1964), 122 ff.
31 Op. cit. pp. 242–3. Cf. also Will, op. cit. I, p. 330.
32 Quoted by Ferguson, op. cit. pp. 261–3.

Chapter 7 Athens and Rome

1 Polybios, V, 27, 1–2.
2 Ferguson, *Hellenistic Athens*, p. 269, n. 4.
3 Cf. Meritt, *Hesperia*, v (1936), 419 ff.
4 Ibid.
5 Will, *Histoire Politique du Monde Hellénistique*, II, p. 111, recalling the
severe judgment of Holleaux (*Rome, la Grèce et les Monarchies
hellénistiques*, pp. 269 ff.) on the assertions of Pausanias (I, 36, 5–6)
concerning an Athenian embassy to Rome; cf. also ibid. p. 112.
6 This is not the place to recall all the controversies raised by the
problem of the Eastern policy of the Roman Senate at the beginning of
the second century B.C. Cf. Will, op. cit. II, pp. 125 ff.
7 Ferguson, op. cit. pp. 276–7.
8 On all these facts see ibid. pp. 312 ff.; Will, op. cit. II, pp. 203 ff.
9 On the Delian cleruchy, cf. the indispensable work by P. Roussel,
Delos, colonie athénienne, 1916.

10 Ibid. Cf. also J. Hatzfeld, *Les Trafiquants italiens dans l'Orient grec*, 1919; Rostovtzeff, *The Social and Economic History of the Hellenistic World*, II, pp. 771 ff.

11 On the problems raised by the disappearance of the cleruchy, see Roussel, op. cit. pp. 51 ff. After 145/4 we find no more decrees issued by Athenians alone, but always by a group consisting of Athenians resident in Delos (invariably named first), *Romaioi, naukleroi* and *emporoi*, and sometimes also *xenoi*; this group has a political character (to award a statue to a magistrate is a political act) but does not constitute a homogeneous whole, politically. Roussel believes that according to circumstances the Assembly might include all those who frequented the gymnasium, or in extreme cases the entire male population.

12 On this point, however, see Roussel's qualifications, op. cit. p. 318, n. 1.

13 Op. cit. p. 427, n. 4.

14 Ibid., p. 429 and n. 2.

15 On this point cf. M. Thompson, 'Ptolemy Philometor and Athens', pp. 119 ff. with reference to the prosperity of Athens after Kynoscephalai.

16 Cf. Will, op. cit. II, p. 183.

17 Cf. J. Travlos, 'The West Side of the Athenian Agora restored', *Hesperia* suppl. viii, Baltimore (1949), 138 ff.; E. Fiandra, 'La Stoa di Attalo nell'Agora ateniese', *Palladio*, n.s. viii (1958), 97–120; R. E. Wycherley, 'The Olympeion of Athens', *Greek, Roman and Byzantine Studies*, v (1964), pp. 161–79.

18 Cf. C. Vatin, *Recherches sur le mariage et la condition de la femme mariée à l'époque hellénistique*, 1970, pp. 125 ff., which cites some examples of mixed marriages in Athens.

19 Ibid. p. 261.

20 Ibid. p. 263.

21 Cf. Marrou, *Histoire de l'Education dans l'Antiquité*, 1948, pp. 284 ff.

22 On the kingdom of Pontus before Mithridates Eupator, cf. Will, op. cit. II, pp. 242 ff. and nn., pp. 392 ff.

23 *OGIS* 368 and 369. On Mithridates the basic work remains that of T. Reinach, *Mithridate Eupator, roi du Pont*, Paris, 1890.

24 Cf. Will, op. cit. pp. 393 ff. and particularly p. 395 for the bibliography in Russian; cf. also Magie, *Roman Rule in Asia Minor*, 1954, pp. 210–20.

25 Poseidonios, ap. Ath. V, 212b and ff. quoted by Ferguson, op. cit. pp. 441–3.

26 Cf. P. Roussel, op. cit. pp. 317 ff.

27 Cf. Roussel, ibid. p. 136 n. 2, citing two inscriptions in which the same man Demodotos is called, in the first, Athenioneus Halaieus and in the second, Aristionos Halaieus. The reference may be to the father or elder brother of the philosopher. Cf. also, for bibliography, Magie, *Roman Rule in Asia Minor*, p. 1106 n. 2.

28 He was none the less awarded honours shortly after: Cf. Raubitschek, 'Sylleia', *Studies for A. C. Johnson*, 1951.

Bibliography

I *Sources*

Students of the late Classical and Hellenistic periods have at their disposal a great wealth and diversity of sources.

Most literary sources have been published and many of them have been very well translated into French (*Collection des Universités de France*) and into English (*Loeb Classical Library*). Jacoby's monumental work, *Die Fragmente der Griechischen Historiker* (1923 onwards) is an inexhaustible source-book, particularly vol. III, part 2. See also *A Commentary on the Ancient Historians of Athens*, 2 vols, Leyden, 1954, and the fragments of comedy collected by J. E. Brill, Leyden, 1958–61.

Epigraphic sources are also abundant and have been subjected to endless commentaries. We recommend the three volumes of Dittenberger's *Sylloge*, 3rd edition by Hiller von Goertringen, 1915–24, and the notes of the *Bulletin épigraphique* published annually in the *Revue des Études Grecques* by J. and L. Robert.

Finally, the contributions of the French School in Athens to the *Bulletin de Correspondance Hellénique*, the reports on the excavations of the Athenian Agora by the American School and on the Belgian excavations at Thorikos (in course of publication: 4 volumes have appeared) and the publications in the *ABSA* enable us, on specific points, to complete our knowledge of the topography and material development of Athens at the end of the Classical period and during the Hellenistic period.

II *Books*

It would be impossible to mention here all books devoted to the history of Athens at the end of the Classical period and during the Hellenistic period. For the fourth century, the student is referred to the bibliography—up until about 1960—in the present writer's *La Fin de*

Bibliography

la Démocratie Athénienne, Paris, P.U.F., 1962. The history of Athens is, of course, central to all general studies of Greek history. Among the most recent we recommend—with certain reservations—that of N. G. Hammond, *A History of Greece to 322 B.C.*, 2nd ed., 1967. In the Hellenistic period the history of Athens becomes less important. For a lucid account of events as a whole, see the important work of E. Will, *Histoire Politique du Monde Hellénistique*, 2 vols, 1966–7, which, moreover, contains an admirable up-to-date bibliography. W. S. Ferguson's *Hellenistic Athens*, London, 1911, although slightly old-fashioned, remains authoritative and has never as yet been replaced.

On the conditions of political life in Athens in the fourth century, two works deserve special mention. One is the collection of articles by R. Sealey, *Essays in Greek Politics*, New York, 1965. The other is the book by Chiara Pecorella Longo, *Eterie e gruppi politici nell'Atene del IV sec. a.c.* Florence, 1971.

No recent contribution has brought new factors to our knowledge of the economic aspect of Athenian history. The trend, however, seems to be towards a less sweeping judgment of the 'crisis' of the fourth century. I have attempted to give an account of this in my book *Histoire d'une Démocratie: Athènes*, Paris, 1971. For contemporary tendencies in the study of the economic and social history of Classical Greece, see two important articles: that of P. Vidal Naquet, 'Economie et Société dans la Grèce ancienne. L'oeuvre de M. I. Finley', *Archives Européennes de Sociologie*, vi (1965) and that of S. C. Humphreys, 'Economy and society in classical Athens', *Annali della Scuola Normale Superiore di Pisa*, series ii, vol. xxxix (1970), 1–26. For the legal aspects of social life, see A. R. W. Harrison, *The Law of Athens*, 2 vols, 1968–71.

As regards Athenian intellectual life, W. Jaeger's great work, *Paideia*, first English edn, 1939–45, remains essential; equally important for a study of religious attitudes is Nilsson's *Geschichte der Griechischen Religion* (*Handbuch der Klassischen Altertumswissenschaft*, v. 1–2), Munich, 1950.

The art of the period is described in two recent volumes by G. Charbonneaux, R. Martin and F. Villard, *Grèce classique* and *Grèce hellénistique*, Paris, Gallimard, 1969–70, where judicious analyses are accompanied by sumptuous illustrations. Finally, an excellent general study of the problems raised by the Hellenistic period is provided by A. Momigliano, 'Introduzione all'Ellenismo', *Rivista Storica Italiana*, lxxxii (1970), 781 ff.

Glossary

AGONOTHETES Supervisors of the games.

ARCHON Supreme magistrate of the *polis*. The eponymous archon gave his name to the year. In the fourth century the powers of the archons decreased considerably.

ATIMOI Citizens deprived of their rights by a legal sentence.

BASILEUS King. In Athens, the archon more particularly responsible for religious affairs.

BOULE Council of 500 members appointed annually.

CLERUCHY A colony of Athenian soldiers established on allied territory. A cleruch received a portion of land (*kleros*) by way of pay.

DECADARCHY Government of ten persons.

DEMOS The body of the citizens.

DIADOCHOI The name given to Alexander's generals who divided up his empire between them after his death.

DIOIKESIS Public administration.

DOKIMASIA Examination.

EKKLESIA The assembly of the *demos*.

ENKTESIS The right to acquire a house or land in Attica, granted to a foreigner.

EPHEBOI, EPHEBEIA Youths doing two years' military service.

EPIDOSIS Voluntary contribution.

EPIMELETES, EPISTATES Supervisors.

ERGASIMA Mines.

GRAPHE (PARANOMON) Action brought for an offence against the laws.

HELIAIA The people's court of Athens.

HIPPARCH Cavalry commander.

ISOTELEIA Equality in tax and tribute.

KATOIKIA Colony.

KOSMETES Magistrate in charge of the epheboi.

LITURGY Public office or duty performed gratuituously by rich Athenians.

METIC Foreigner resident in Attica and paying residence tax.

MISTHOPHORIA Remuneration for public office.

Glossary

MISTHOS EKKLESIASTIKOS Salary paid to Athenian magistrates and, in the fourth century, to all those attending the sessions of the Assembly.

NOMOPHYLAQUES Guardians of the law.

NOMOTHETES Legislators and jurists responsible for drawing up laws.

OIKOUMENE The inhabited world.

ORGEONES Members of the same religious association.

PHOROS Tribute.

POLETAI Vendors of public property.

POLIS The city-state as a community.

PROSTATES Patron (for a metic, the citizen who represents him and stands guarantor for him before the courts).

PROXENIA Official status of persons representing the interests of a foreign state in their own community.

PRYTANY The period (about 1/10 of a year) during which each of the 10 *phylae* (tribes) presided in turn over the Council and ekklesia.

PYLAGORIA Deputies from a city-state to the Amphiktyonic Council at Delphi.

SITONAI Commissioners responsible for buying corn.

SOPHRONISTAI Superintendents of the youth in the gymnasia at Athens; there were 10 of them.

STRATEGOI Magistrates whose functions were essentially military.

SYCOPHANT Accuser, informer.

SYMMACHIA Military alliance.

SYMMORIA Group of tax-payers.

SYNEDRION Council of the allies of Athens.

SYNKECHOREMENA Newly exploited mines.

TAMIAS EPI TEN DIOIKESIN Treasurer of the administration.

THEORIKON Right of entry to the theatre.

THEOROI Sacred ambassadors.

THETES Citizens of the lowest class in the census.

THIASOI Religious associations.

TRIERARCHY The most costly of the liturgies; it involved arming and equipping a trireme.

TYRANT A usurper who seized power in certain Greek city-states, generally posing as defender of the people against the aristocracy.

Index

Index

Index

Index

Index